Sickened

DATE	EYE 1	ENT 2	NECK 3	CHEST 4	HEART 5	ABD 6	G.U. 7

12-6-78

S - Mother relates that over past se
has been Cx of intermittent sore thr
has still not been good but has been
past few yrs. Over the past 48 hrs.
of the throat becoming more sore, gl
swollen and been Cx of H/A almost da
recent opthalmology exam in which he
to be the right prescription and was
wearing them. Also relates to some
Has had no nausea, vomiting or diarr
of some generalized abd. discomfort.
running a low grade temp. over the p
being more than 99.4 - 99.6.

O - Does not appear in any acute di
        Bilat/ TM's clear and intact.
clear. There is no rhinorrea. There
a 1+ tonsilar enlarg. with extreme e
patchy yellow exudate bilat. There
small ant. cerv. node lymphadenopath
tender.
        GROM, no rigidity.
                Clear to A & P. Go
sounds. Good expansion.
                    Reg. sinus rhyt
88.   Soft, n
organomegly or tenderness.
out rashes. Warm and color is good.

Sickened

The Memoir of a Munchausen by Proxy Childhood

Julie Gregory

Foreword by
MARC D. FELDMAN, M.D.

CENTURY · LONDON

Published by Century in 2004

1 3 5 7 9 10 8 6 4 2

Copyright © Julie Gregory 2003

Julie Gregory has asserted her right under the Copyright,
Designs and Patents Act, 1988 to be indentified as the author of this work

This novel is a work of non fiction. The events it recounts are true;
many are documented. Most names outside the family have been changed
to protect the innocent and the guilty.

First published in the United Kingdom in 2004 by Century
The Random House Group Limited
20 Vauxhall Bridge Road, London SW1V 2SA

First published in the United States in 2003 by Bantam Dell,
A division of Random House, Inc.
Published simultaneously in Canada

Random House Australia (Pty) Limited
20 Alfred Street, Milsons Point, Sydney,
New South Wales 2061, Australia

Random House New Zealand Limited
18 Poland Road, Glenfield,
Auckland 10, New Zealand

Random House South Africa (Pty) Limited
Endulini, 5A Jubilee Road, Parktown 2193, South Africa

The Random House Group Limited Reg. No. 954009

www.randomhouse.co.uk

A CIP catalogue record for this book is available from
the British Library

Papers used by Random House are natural, recyclable products made from
wood grown in sustainable forests. The manufacturing processes conform to
the environmental regulations of the country of origin

ISBN 1 844 13442 3

Design by Glen Edelstein

Printed and bound in Great Britain by
Mackays of Chatham Plc, Chatham, Kent

Foreword

MUNCHAUSEN BY PROXY may be the single most complex—and lethal—form of maltreatment known today. It is formally defined as the falsification or induction of physical and/or emotional illness by a caretaker of a dependent person. In most cases, the perpetrator is a mother and the victim is her own child. Baron Karl von Münchhausen was a real historical figure, a soldier and an adventurer of the eighteenth century who became notorious for his outrageous stories. In 1951, a British physician borrowed the baron's name and introduced the term *Munchausen syndrome* for people who feign or produce illness in themselves to gain sympathy, nurturance, and control over others. In turn, MBP was coined to describe those who use a substitute or "proxy" for the same reasons. It is conservatively estimated that 1,200 new cases of MBP are reported annually in the United States, with proportional numbers in other countries based on their populations. However, many more cases go unreported—indeed, entirely undetected—due to the covert nature of the maltreatment. A recent study indicates that when a case of MBP is finally recognized, up to twenty-five percent of the sickened child's siblings have already died—most likely earlier victims of the perpetrator. Only when the same pattern of symptoms appears in the second child of the family, or the third or fourth or fifth, have professionals and legal authorities been forced to realize that motherhood can twist into a strange illness-related type of abuse that, unlike battering or sexual violation, defies ready categorization. Even though the FBI has been vigilantly aware of MBP for several years, Munchausen by proxy is still a public health tragedy that, paradoxically, has been largely hidden from the public.

I entered the strange world of MBP begrudgingly. Having been primarily interested in Munchausen syndrome, I was reluctant to enter the difficult and troubling arena of child neglect and abuse. However, being a "Munchausen" expert meant attempting to master its variants; it meant wading into the waters of child protection despite the fact that MBP perpetrators almost invariably deny their actions, even when caught on tape. I have since consulted and testified nationally in numerous MBP cases, often before judges and juries who are dubious that such a bizarre form of abuse can even exist. I have discussed the syndrome in my own books and in chapters for books by others, and have answered over a thousand related inquiries through telephone, mail, and e-mail. I have worked in the field of MBP essentially every day for over a decade, and it still breaks my heart.

One day, while trolling the Internet for links to expand my website, I came across a new and important perspective on MBP. A woman named Julie Gregory had launched her own site where she shared aspects of her MBP victimization through vivid writing and moving photographs. She described her interest in writing a book and I e-mailed my encouragement, thus beginning a relationship that has culminated here.

In *Sickened*, we get an unprecedented look into the experience of MBP. There are over five hundred clinical articles and books on the subject, but until now no one has told the full story of MBP from the inside. Julie Gregory grew up not in a playground among friends, but in the weirdly structured and antiseptic world of doctors' offices and hospitals. Her life was completely focused on the falsely constructed world of her various "illnesses," and the caregivers and doctors who might have nurtured her were co-opted into damaging both her body and her soul. Indeed, doctors are the unwitting accomplices in MBP, conditioned to have blind faith in what they are told by patients and families. It is undeniable that what a parent says is usually the best guide to what's wrong with the child, so it takes an enormous shift in attitude for a physician to accept that the stories ring untrue, that the test results are normal, that no treatment ever works, that no amount of testing is ever "enough," and that the parent is more accurately called a perpetrator. Of course, the best lies are the ones that mix fact and fiction: children can show real symptoms, yet how they are created can remain conveniently undisclosed.

A parent can be ruthless in her quest to garner emotional satisfaction from the ailments of her child. She needn't be highly educated, only persuasive. If MBP perpetrators find that interest is waning in their drama of "selfless" caretaking, they can move on to new audiences: new hospitals, new emergency rooms. They often scour textbooks or the Internet for medical information to enhance performances that could put any good actress to shame.

As Julie got older, it might seem to the reader that she colluded with her mother in misleading doctors. Did she? Never. She was simply overpowered. How can a child counter a mother's total self-absorption, an impenetrable world that is a whole unto itself? We know that even adult MBP victims may not disclose the true sources of their illnesses out of fear of abandonment or punishment if they stop being sick. Other elements creep into the MBP picture, such as *Stockholm syndrome*, epitomized by Patty Hearst's adopting the cause of her violent abductors: Children often protect their abusers and resist making revelations to the very medical and social service personnel who could rescue them.

Sickened does not consist of unreliable memories recovered through hypnosis or a therapist's leading questions, but of events that were never forgotten—a blessing and a curse for Julie. They were further validated by Julie's compiling the whole messy, disturbing stack of her medical records. It is from these records that we see how easily a mother's lies became insidiously transformed into medical fact.

Julie Gregory has a remarkable story to tell and a remarkable fortitude to share. She is also lucky to be alive. Author Philip Yancey has written, "Life is not a problem to be solved but a work to be made, and that work may well utilize much raw material we would prefer to do without." Julie has a resilience only scarcely imaginable under the circumstances. That she has emerged not only with her sense of self intact but with enough clarity to write about it is amazing. I hope that her putting her life to paper in this searing and beautiful memoir can silence some of the demons of the past and help those still caught in the web of MBP maltreatment.

I expect *Sickened* to ignite a powder keg that brings MBP forever out of the closet, giving off a light that doctors, health care organizations, professional groups, child abuse workers, and the general public can never again ignore. Born of one of the darkest and most intractable of childhood situations, the words assembled here represent a monument, a genuine triumph of the human spirit.

Marc D. Feldman, M.D.
Department of Psychiatry and
Behavioral Neurobiology,
University of Alabama, Tuscaloosa

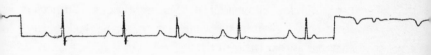

THE PART I HATED most was the shaving.
I mean, if you're a twelve-year-old
girl, how much hair can you have on your chest? But
they'd lather me up anyway and run a new plastic Bic
between my barely-there breasts. They needed me
smooth and hairless so the little white pads would stick
to those points constellated around my heart and record
my beats. And while they were preparing, I'd hover
above myself, intent on studying the nubby white ceiling
tiles, imagining a room where I lived, inverted, upon the
ceiling, away from the clutter of our trailer, away from
the hospital—just floating in pure, white peace.

The scent of the shaving cream pulls me back down
from the ceiling: It's the same kind Dad used. Every day
before dawn, he'd erupt in violent heaving and crawl off
to the toilet trying to peel the Agent Orange from his
lungs. Sometimes the sounds of his retching would come
out the mouths of those elusive figures in my dreams, the
worlds between sleep and wake merging seamlessly for a
few groggy moments. He'd usually shave after he puked.

In an unspoken understanding, the examining room nurse folds a giant pile of cream from the can onto her palm, so much that as she smooths an inch-thick trail down my chest, our naked skin never touches.

Eventually the tide of Agent Orange would ebb and he'd lean dizzy in the doorway and say, "I'm selling Buicks, Sissy. Get it? Selling Buicks? Buuicck. Buuuuiiick." Then he'd cackle and brush the back of his meaty fist across his mouth.

The nurse picks up a new blue-handled blade and runs it neatly down my sternum, slicing out another clean, pink row.

And what do you do at seven in the morning but laugh with your big, lumbering father, who's pretending the doorway of the bathroom is a lamppost and that he, leaning on it like a drunk, is hawking Buicks in his best barker accent?

And then they're done. The white pads have been spread with a clear magnetic jelly and pressed on to six different locations. Their wires run into one larger river of wires that flows from under my sternum down my abdomen, emerging out the zipper of my pants like I had some elaborate cable TV pay-per-view setup in there. The rubber-coated electrodes feed into a tape recorder that fits snugly into a rectangular leather harness; it looks like a purse. I wear the strap over my shoulder, and while my seventh-grade life ticks away, so do the heartbeats that go with it, right into the box.

For starters, I was a sick kid. Bean-pole skinny and as fragile as a micro-wave soufflé, I bruised easy and wilted in a snap. Kids in school used to walk straight up to me and ask point-blank if I was anorexic. But I wasn't; just sick. And Mom bent over backwards trying to find out what was wrong with me. It wasn't just that I had a heart problem. It was everything rolled into one, bleeding together with so many indistinguishable layers that to get to the root of it was impossible, like peeling off every transparent layer of an onion, and when I got old enough to peel the onion myself, every layer made me cry.

I was conceived in the sickly womb of a sickly mother—who starved herself and in turn starved me. She was highly anemic and blind with toxemia at the time of my birth—the result, she explained, of high blood pressure cutting off the circulation to her eyes. I was pushed into this world premature at three pounds seven ounces, an embryonic little bird, glowing translu-cently, and when they slapped me I didn't even yowl. They thought I was dead. The doctor, holding my bluish body upside down by the ankles, took one look at me and said, "My, what big feet she has." And then I was ushered into an incubator where I lay, as all embryonic creatures do, waiting to hatch into the real world, out-side the bubble. After that, my health only balanced pre-cariously on the edge of a "Let's get to the bottom of what's wrong with this kid" kind of existence.

There were early nose-'n'-throat flare-ups, loud belching that defied my delicate appearance, pesky and persistent migraines, swollen tonsils that fluttered a plea for removal whenever I said "Ahhh," a deviated septum blamed for my mouth hanging open to breathe, and elusive allergies that forever deprived me of sustenance from the four basic food groups. As we got closer to pinning down my mysterious illness in the cardiology department, Mom moved into micromanaged health care with the logistical vigor of a drill sergeant.

"Look, dammit, this kid is sick, all right? Just look at her. And so help me God, if she dies on me because you can't find anything wrong with her, I'll sue you for every cent you got." Mom's face was long, her eyes diving into slits, and she had that little white blob of thick spit that always played on her bottom lip whenever she got upset. Her voice trailed after any doctor who said no more tests could be done, stalked him down the corridor, sliced through the silence of the hallway.

"Jeesus Christ," she hissed, returning to the examining room, "I cannot believe that incompetent son of a bitch."

"Don't worry, Mom. It's okay. We'll go find another one."

This is how I offered reassurance, by telling her we'd just keep going.

"Look, I'm trying to help you with this, sacrificing my life to find out what the hell is wrong with you. So stop fucking it up when we get in here by acting all normal. Show them how sick you are and *let's get to the bottom of this*, okay?"

"Okay."

WE LIVED TOGETHER day in and day out—me, Mom, Dad, little Danny, and then later, the foster kids—but Dad never knew I was getting my chest shaved. He was summoned by

Mom with a set of "decent clothes" and the boxed white loafers only when a demonstration of fatherly support was paramount at a hospital. Otherwise, he was left to his back-to-back reruns of *M*A*S*H*, his red-stained pistachio fingers and mounds of empty nut carcasses piled high on his belly.

We lived in a double-wide trailer then, stuck on the dead end of a dirt road in a backwoods patch of Ohio; a wild, woolly green, lushed-out part of the country with roller coaster hills that held their breath in a *Deliverance* kind of way. I swear you could almost hear the banjos folded faintly into the breeze.

My parents had hauled their black velvet painting of Jesus crucified, with the 3-D blood from the crown of thorns blobbing down the side of his head, all the way from Arizona and then through the six other places we'd lived until we settled in the holler of Burns Road.

Our living room was outfitted with an early imitation-wagon-wheel velour sofa set, and Jesus hung against the burnt-orange velvet wallpaper, which had been pasted over wood paneling, so that the grooves showed through as darkened, hollow stripes. Sticky shag (as if someone had vacuumed up honey) swayed like undulating seaweed across the floor. Miniature concrete farm animals dotted our yard in pairs and groups—white baby chicks, mini cows with pink udders, roosters a-courting hens, a donkey in a sombrero—and when we were in town for my doctors' appointments, Mom always kept an eagle eye out for additions to her barnyard collection.

I remember my dad then, manateelike; big, soft, scrubbed clean as if he'd just been run through a car wash on a La-Z-Boy gurney. Naked white skin stretched taut over an enormous belly, the pallor of sick clay. No hearing. No sight. No opinion. The dark living room of our trailer held nothing——except sporadic uproarious laughter to the endless hijinks of Hawkeye and Hunnicut.

Once, when I was seven, I lay in bed drifting to sleep when Dad roared, "Siiissy! Siiisssssy!" I leapt out of bed, thinking "FIRE," and tore down the hall in slippery full-footed pajamas.

"Fix me some toast, will ya?" Dad's fingers placidly folded over his chest, thick calves propped up on the snapping-turtle hinges of the recliner footrest, he never took his eyes off the set.

Aside from trips to the doctor, we mostly stayed home in that trailer on the dead end of a dirt road, and there was a great gulf between how we really were and how we looked when we got out. I have a photo from when I was about eleven and Danny, my brother, was just four, when we drove up to Niagara Falls for a vacation. We're in a fake wooden barrel that looks like it was careening over the side of the falls, and we each wear a smile that couldn't have been more plastic than the water swirling around us. I am naturally blond by Clairol, wearing the latest in JCPenney pastels, and exuding happiness.

But happiness is relative when you're twelve, sitting in a chrome-on-steel examination room, goose bumps giving you that plucked-chicken look, with a nubbly paper sheet tucked into your clammy armpits. Until now the answers had run like whispers over the hills just ahead of us. A little intermittent tachycardia here, some Marfanoid habitus there. Never anything code-red enough to get me completely, legitimately diagnosed. But they kept looking. Because Mom was positive that the answer was right there in my heart. A mother knows these things. She's the one who'd see me go ashy in the face, she's the one who'd take my skipping pulse, and she's the one who watched the weight fall right off my bones, all the while my height skyrocketed. So that's what flamed us onwards, after the answer. It was right there, just always right there before us, waiting to be sussed out, and then it would all make sense. And in some ways, she was right. But time might be running out for me, so when Mom insisted on another test and they wouldn't do it, well, that's when we'd get the hell out of there and try to find somebody who knew what they were doing.

MY MOTHER, SANDY SUE SMITH, was married off by her mother at the tender age of seventeen to a man in his fifties named Smokey, who kept a carnival act on the edge of town. Smokey was a small, tight man with crisp tabs of sideburns that sliced down from under his curled black cowboy hat. He had trick riding horses, horses trained for the carnival ring, and he taught Sandy Sue to do outrageously dangerous stunts with names like "The Apache Flyaway" and "Lay Over the Neck." After the stunts, Smokey would strap Sandy to a pegged wooden wheel, set it spinning, and throw nineteen-inch-long knives at her. And then there she'd be, having survived the ten sharp blades that jutted haphazardly from the cracked wood around her, smiling brightly with one leg cocked, like a model, a dainty hand flipped above in triumph. This was before she had me but I've seen the pictures and they are stunning: She stands tall upon the bare back of a wild, white horse blurring across a field, with a ruby-tangerine-streaked sky as the backdrop.

In another photo Smokey is snapping a twenty-five-foot braided leather bullwhip out toward Sandy, who stands pinned to the horse trailer with an expressionless face, the whip side-winding like a snake about to coil around her throat. They wear matching outfits of black-and-white yoked satin shirts with pearl snap buttons, silver conchs sewn down their trouser seams, and belt buckles the size of serving platters.

How Sandy ended up with Smokey goes something like this: She has a mother and a father and an older brother named Lee, who is a little *off*, wink, wink. The father ignores the family, keeps his attention on a gun collection stashed throughout the house. The mother, Madge, is from a clan of West Virginians who sleep with their own brothers and sisters and have cross-eyed children to prove it. Sandy is occasionally left with men that do terrible things to her in a shadowy basement. The father with the guns is replaced one day by another gun-toting father—only this time with a badge. He makes Sandy ride behind him on his motorcycle with his hand curved around and resting on her bare leg. He takes her to remote fishing holes with tall grass and the occasional fisherman who looks the other way. Two years later, Sandy walks in from school to find this new dad has stuck a gun in his mouth and blown himself apart right there on the living room sofa.

Madge has a tenth-grade education and has never worked a day in her life. There is scarcely ever food in the house. Sandy's given no lunch money and by the time she's fifteen, she's famished. Sinking in on herself with malnutrition, she collapses on one of the floors she scrubs with ammonia after school. In the hospital she lies with pelvic bones poking through thin white sheets, while they feed her three meals a day. When she's strong enough to be discharged, Madge gives her to Smokey, a man who lives down the road with horses and a farm, a man who can take care of her as well as he does his own cattle. And she climbs into his truck with going-to-girls'-town enthusiasm, lured by the promise of her very own horse. Off she goes with a man. It is all she's known.

Years go by with Sandy strapped to the wheel: white leather, showgirl's smile. Coal black hair separated down the middle into leather tunnels that lace up the side in Indian squaw fashion, accentuating the trace of Cherokee blood that gives her the high cheekbones and blushed full lips. She runs alongside as her gift horse tumbles into a full gallop, grips its long, flying mane, and then, clutching the horn, springs into the saddle with a panther's grace, pushing to balance her way up until she is standing tall while the spectators cheer. Still running at a breakneck speed, she plunges under the horse's belly and thrusts her arm out in performance-style splendor, ta-daaaaa. This is the Russian Death Drag. She has captured an audience and, for the first time in her existence, something other than a life, a body full of pain.

IT IS DURING ONE OF OHIO'S BRUTAL WINTERS that Smokey comes down with his annual bad cold and Sandy has her psychic premonition. When Smokey wasn't out on summer tour traveling behind the Grand Ole Opry with his act, he was working double shifts down at the Swan dry cleaning factory, sucking in the rich chemical-laden steam. And he usually got sick every winter. But no matter how hard he hacked or how many specks of blood flew out with a spit, there was no way in hell Smokey was going to go to any quack doctor at Sandy's insistence. Ain't nothing ever wrong with Smokey that a swig of Pepto-Bismol couldn't fix. So when he woke up close to Christmas the color of dirty mop water, he had Sandy run into town to pick him up some. That burn in his chest was probably just indigestion, same as it ever was. All the while Sandy was driving, she wanted to keep on going, to never come back. She saw in her mind's eye walking in to find Smokey cold and stiff, his face frozen in pain, and she didn't want to come home to another man dead. She drove round and round curvy country roads, frantically thinking of someone to call. But she had nobody but Smokey. When she did pull in a few hours later, Smokey was standing in the gravel driveway, as pissed as a bear with a sore ass, chomping at the bit over his Christmas dinner being late. They climbed into bed that night around ten and not a half hour into sleep did Smokey bolt upright and let out a bloodcurdling scream, go into a death rattle, and fall back stiff onto the depression of the pillows.

Sandy was left with horses and bills, a mortgage on the new ranch, and loads of tack: show bridles, saddles, blankets, and brushes. And, despite what sounds like a marriage arranged in hell, she loved Smokey. He treated her better than any man she'd ever known, if only by the baseline that he never beat her. Now, not only has she not got him but she's got no insurance, no money, no job, no family. She sells the horses and the knife-throwing wheel, the saddles and the tack, just to afford a casket for the man no one comes to see. Sandy stands alone at Smokey's funeral in a nameless parlor, wailing over his body until the undertaker ushers her out when the rental time is up. She is twenty-six.

Now. Somewhere across town is a smiling scrawny nineteen-year-old kid, freshly turned loose from the Vietnam War, having done a few questionable things to land himself in a VA hospital. He wears a permanent Westside look carved on his face from years of beatings by a father more interested in raising tomatoes in the backyard than his kids, a wary expectant look so that if somebody, anybody, looked back too closely or for too long, then *he* knew that *they* knew something he didn't want them to know and it was either fight or run. Usually fight. He took that look into Vietnam, where he got a lung full of Agent Orange and then watched through it as his best friend from high school exploded beside him in the brush. He held his friend's broken head in his hands and wrung bottled-up, exhausted sobs from his own. Four months later he walked free from the war, with a low white buzz between his ears, out into the sun from the VA psych ward with only a mild and questionable case of paranoid schizophrenia. This is my Dad, Dan Gregory the First. His actual time spent in Vietnam itself added up to only a few months.

Sandy and Dan bumped into each other soon afterward in the parking lot of the gas station where he worked, and they rushed one another with a hunger so penetrating it came to cannibalize their very souls. Sandy pulled in for gas at the Lane and Sullivan service station and took a sharp turn in her life by asking the mechanic on duty to check her oil. My father got in her car and never got out. They held court for three months, then tied the knot. Tight. Dad wanted to get married Catholic, and the priest sat Sandy down and said, "Do you realize this man is crazy, my child? He's crazy."

She'd later say she had no idea he'd been in the psych ward at all and chalked up her nineteen years with him as a learning experience. Funny, there were just as many years with Dan as there were inches in the knives Smokey threw at her.

NOW. IT IS ONE THING to see the VA papers that say your dad is crazy, to hear constantly regurgitated bits from your mom confirming that he's crazy, and how he got that way. It is a different thing entirely to walk away from this scene, to look back years later and wonder if perhaps the woman who is your mother is actually crazier than the man who is your father—only without the paperwork to back it up.

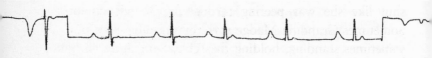

M Y FIRST MEMORIES of medical may-
hem began when we moved to
Arizona to be closer to Grandma Madge, Mom's mom. I
was three then, with long wispy hair the shade of banana taffy, pulled to a shine. I enjoyed the rich life of a
three-year-old: roller skates strapped over my shoes and
a pillow belted to my butt, frying an egg on the sidewalk
in midday Phoenix heat, learning cuss words in Spanish
from the Mexican boy next door, and visiting Grandma,
who lived just up the street.

By then Grandma Madge was a born-again Chris-
tian and devout basement Sunday school teacher. She
wore a fishing cap with a smiley face on it to match her
own cheerful self, and would take me down to the lake
on sweltering Phoenix afternoons to catch sunfish. On
the way, we'd drive along the mountains, their tops
shrouded by the pollution haze that hung over Phoenix
and bled out into the desert. As we'd come up on Encino
Mountain, the largest peak, Grandma would lurch the
sedan over on the dusty roadside and, with a hand

shielding her eyes like a visor, scan the mountaintop haze for signs of Jesus. Once she spotted him, she'd tug me over onto her lap so I could pop my little body out the driver-side window and share the revelation.

"See him, Jewelly?" She'd thrust a wrinkled finger past my head. "He's *right* there." She'd squeeze an eye half shut like she was peering through a rifle viewfinder. Sometimes Grandma Madge saw him kneeling in prayer, sometimes standing, holding the Bible. Sometimes she'd squeak out a few tears from the sheer beauty of his majesty. Then she'd start jabbing again with her finger. "Can't you see him, Jewelly? He's *right* there, right *there*!"

Uh-uh, Grandma, I don't think I can. But Grandma Madge got so exasperated at my lack of vision that I began to guess at his wardrobe from fractured memories of Sunday school pictures.

"Oh, Grandma, is that him in the brown dress? With the baby goat? Ohhh, now I think I see."

Grandma Madge shuddered in rapture as soon as I started talking about his lace-up sandals. But then she'd suddenly clamp down on my little arms and swing me around to direct fire of her rotten breath.

"Did you really see Jesus up there?" she'd say. "You're not lying now, are you? 'Cause liars go straaaiiiight to hell," the "straight" reverberating from the very depths of what to me seemed like the black pit of hell right then and there. This is the only time Grandma Madge got mad at me, when I lied about seeing Jesus at the top of Encino Mountain, living up there in the industrial wastelands of outer Phoenix. So I started seeing him a little sooner and memorizing details from Sunday school that started to convince even me, until I could have sworn that the rock I laid my lies upon under

Grandma Madge's pointing finger actually took on the shape of that bearded man in prayer.

SO WE'D GET ON DOWN to the lake and lounge on the smooth rocks and catch fish with prickly parts wherever I'd touch. "Sun fish," she called them, because they glistened in the light bouncing off the lake. There's a photo of me standing there knock-kneed with a scrunched-up smile that shone no less than the sun itself, holding a fishing pole high over my head with a spiky little fish flopping on the end of the line. We always gave those little fish their freedom and that was my favorite part: handing them over to Grandma to peel the hook out of their mouths and then, squatting down at water's edge, watching them swim away. As for the ones that floated on top, I'd hope and pray to Jesus that they were as okay as Grandma said they were right after she crunched the hook out of the side of their face.

Then the sun would sink a little, feathering lightly into the surface of the water, and Grandma and I would climb back in the car and go off and get in a car wreck.

It was never anything too serious. A head-on here, a rear-ending there, always at slow speed and usually with old people like her. Kind of like bumper cars, only the real thing. Sometimes she'd say, "Here we go, Jewelly," which meant to scoot over and clutch the door handle, squinching your eyes shut. Her targets were usually red things: signs and brake lights. When she'd smash into another driver, she'd hop out of the car and disappear, melting into the small pool of people who were starting to gather.

I'd crawl out my open door (Grandma was always kind enough to stretch across the seat and open it for me from the inside before she got out) and wander around in the confusion. Usually some stranger would be shocked to find me at the scene of an accident, standing in the buzz of an intersection not knowing what part of the puzzle my piece fit. They'd scoop me up, fussing and full of questions, and carry me into a 7-Eleven or a bait-and-tackle shop or their own house, and eventually my mother would come to pick me up.

Grandma was never taken to the hospital or injured in any real way; she got in these wrecks to talk to people. Standing in the middle of the street, she'd fish through her giant white textured leatherette purse—perched on the knee of her leg hoisted up to the wheel well—for her wallet, and show them the pictures of her four-year-old granddaughter who was with her—the four-year-old that no one seemed to notice was missing.

Even though Grandma's happiness at the scene of an accident was effervescent, she eventually got hauled away. The officer stood before her like a stone effigy and lectured on the dangers of her constant and questionable benders, and Grandma Madge just smiled, God-blessed him, and climbed into the back of the police car on her own, fingering her white Bible like a Persian lap cat. So Grandma lost her license, and got forbidden to ever stick me in a car and drive off anywhere again, but she still came over to baby-sit me when Mom and Dad went out on dates.

W HILE MOM GETS DRESSED, Dad sits me on his knee and bounces me up and down: "Joe, Joe broke his toe, riding on a buff-a-lo." I toss my long hair and giggle. "Daaad! I'm not Joe, I'm Jewelly!"

I adore my father. He takes me out to 7-Eleven and grabs a Clark Bar off the shelf. He rips it open and gives me half, then lets the empty wrapper fall from his hand as softly as a feather and we walk out the door, climb into our little peanut-mobile and roar off, giggling the whole way home.

On baby-sitting nights, Grandma and I play Chutes and Ladders or Candy Land. We take a Mr. Bubble bath and just before bed she digs around and pulls something out from the depths of her bottomless purse: clusters of sticky, fused-together Cracker Jacks that taste funny, or some strange warped candy melded to its wrapper. Turning down your grandmother's candy is a breach of etiquette even a four-year-old knows better than to commit, so I'd sit at the kitchen table and nibble on whatever strange concoction she put in front of me, feigning "mmmmm"s while she watched. And when I was through, she'd start in asking.

"Honey, do you feel all right? You're looking a little peak-id."

I feel fine as I slide my hand down a shimmery wall-papered hall, heading to my room for jammies. Grandma Madge follows, muttering her thoughts out loud. "Oh, honey, I'm worried. You look so sick. C'mere, let Grandma feel your forehead." She flips my blond bangs out of the way and lays her icy knuckles against my face.

"Oh, God, Jewelly, you are burning up, just burning up. I better call the squad." Grandma is serious, her face etched in worry and hovering inches from mine. Her fingers spread my eyelids apart, looking for signs that she can report to the hospital. Maybe I am feeling something in my tummy. Maybe I do have a fever. *What does it feel like, Grandma? Am I sick, Grandma?*

"Oh, honey, you are so sick. But let's just wait till your mother comes home. Then we'll all go to the hospital. I'd take you now, but your daddy won't let me. I think you'll live until they get home. I hope so, honey." She pats my head while she shakes her own.

"Let us pray now." And Grandma Madge puts her hand in mine and bows her head. I start bawling. I don't want to die. But Grandma's not sure if I'll make it. My stomach is twisted like a braid. I'm propped on cushions against my headboard, just like the ninety-year-old lady down the street, who faded into her pillows and died last year.

Grandma asks me again about the sharp pains in my tummy and my hand slips under the covers to hold myself. I'm afraid to breathe in too much. I'm watching Grandma pace back and forth, back and forth between me and the phone: She picks it up, calls the squad, hangs up when they answer. She winds the curly phone cord around her finger, pulls it out, peeks out my curtains, feels my forehead, runs back to the phone, picks it up to listen for the dial tone, sets it down.

And then soft headlights ease into the drive. The car creeps into the garage, the engine cuts. Mom and Dad slip quietly in the front door and Madge flicks on the foyer light switch, rushing them, blurting out that I've eaten something that looked funny and how a strange man had come to the house and given her the Cracker Jacks as a gift and she thought it was okay because he seemed like a *nice* black man and he didn't look like he would do anything poisonous or with razor blades like you hear about these days.

Grandma Madge clasps her hands to her chest like a praying mantis, her voice a bird, pulled higher and higher by a string.

It takes a few seconds for Mom and Dad, with steady blinking, to decipher her words. And as they sink in, Mom explodes, "My Gawd! How could you, Madge? What the hell is wrong with you? She's a little girl. How could you give her candy from a black man?"

Dad surveys the two of them for a minute, scanning between their faces like a slow-motion tennis match. Then he drops his head to his chest, lets out a long whizzing hiss, and tromps past us to bed. He was twenty-five then.

Mom is frantic, running through the house, grabbing things to take to the hospital in case they have to keep me, *in case I don't make it,* and barking out orders to Grandma Madge.

And then suddenly, I'm scooped up from behind, bundled in a blanket, and raced to the car. We veer around corners and punch through lights on our way to the hospital. Occasionally Mom leans over and whispers, "Check on her," and Grandma Madge flops a saggy arm back and gropes at the blanket to make sure it's rising and falling with each of my breaths.

Clunking into park in the ER lot, as Grandma sits on the shadowy side of the car, gathering her enormous purse, Mom turns around to face me in the backseat. With the yellow lamplight casting a jack-o'-lantern glow on her long face, she reaches back and smooths out the folds in my pajamas, her eyes latching on to mine.

"Now, honey, I need you to show the doctor how sick you were back at the house, okay? I don't want him sending you home if there's a razor blade stuck inside you."

A ND IT WAS AFTER FIVE TRIPS to the ER that Dad finally said, "That Madge is a fucking *battleac*! We're going back to Ohio." And so we loaded black velvet Jesus into the U-Haul and drove far away from the battleac pandemonium of Grandma Madge. And along the way, over the empty highways that in the 1970s still stretched between the desert and the sparse rolling hills of the Midwest, I'd sit on Mom's lap and rummage through her purse.

"You looking for the suckers, honey? Here, let me get 'em for you."

Mom pulls out a new book of matches and carefully bends back the cover to expose two fresh red rows of the minipops she's been giving me for as long as I can remember. My mouth waters when I see their shimmery crimson tips. The first one is always the best, and I pluck it out and get it fast on my tongue, waiting for the metallic zolt to rush my taste buds. Once the hardest layer dissolves, I flip the match against the side of my teeth and crunch the softer bits off the stick, spitting the white flimsy paper to the floor, swallowing the rest.

One by one, I devour the pack, trying to finish it off for Mom. Mom pulls out a hairbrush and strokes my long blond hair; my crown bobs toward her with each pull of the brush. She smiles softly at me with a sucker in my mouth as Dad clenches the wheel, lost in thought, driving us as fast and as far away as he can from the crafty antics of a madwoman named Madge.

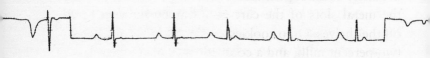

"SO WHAT I'VE NOTICED, Dr. Phillips, is that Julie is mostly sick on schooldays and has a soaring fever and really bad sore throats. I think it might be strep or tonsillitis."

OHIO IS HOME NOW, and after enough moves to shuffle me through five different kindergartens, we've finally settled into a swanky rural suburb, thanks to Dad landing a steady job with full benefits at the Rickenbacker Air Force Base.

These are the salad years: white two-story house, baby blue carpeting, sunken den, bay windows with furry African violet leaves curled up on the sill, hot with diffused sunlight streaming in through freshly Windexed double-paned glass.

And now that we've got full medical coverage, Mom's got to get me established with a pediatrician. Township Family Physicians lies about ten miles down the road from us. Since my first checkup, I've been back for sore throats, nausea, and headaches. Mom thinks

I'm allergic to the new carpeting in our house, but Dr. Phillips puts me on an elimination diet to see if it's something I'm eating. He tells her to take chocolate, meat, eggs, dairy, and bread out of every meal I eat.

After our appointment, Mom and I amble down the aisles of the supermarket, my fingers looped through the metal slots of the cart as I watch what she pulls off the shelves: Oreo cookies, pork chops, Grade A eggs, two-percent milk, and a couple loaves of Wonder. Bay's Grocery doesn't seem to have any of the foods Dr. Phillips wants me to eat.

Today, I'm back at Township, getting seen for my headaches. Mom and I sit in the examining room, waiting for the doctor.

"How do you act when you're sick, Julie? Show me." I slouch on the edge of the table, limbs dangling. I hang my tongue out and my bottom lip falls away from my teeth like a *National Geographic* pygmy with a lip plate in.

"That's right. Now what do you think the doctor is going to say if he comes in here and you're sitting up and all smiling? Do you think he's going to believe me that you're sick? You got to show him how sick you are outside the doctor's office. We got to get to the bottom of this thing so Mommy can get some rest." She licks her thumb and smudges dried egg from the side of my mouth. Her spit smells like rot.

"Okay, honey?"

"Okay, Mommy."

"So, you say Julie's been running a fever, Ms. Gregory, along with some sore throats?" Dr. Phillips leans easy against his sink counter, scribbling notes on my chart.

NAME	Gregory, Julie							# 1798.18		DATE OF BIRTH 5/6

DATE 1978	EYE 1	ENT 2	NECK 3	CHEST 4	HEART 5	ABD 6	G.U. 7	MUSC SKEL 8	NERV 9	SKIN 10	ASSESSMENT	PLAN
4-6	cc: Sore throat, dry cough, ears hurt											
54#	back of neck hurts. Fever - 102° since											
T-101.4	S- 2D Hx severe sore throat, cough, fever to 102										Pharangitis prob. strep	Pen VK 250 qid
	O - TM's clear, throat very hyperemic including											fluids, rest,
	uvula, no exudate, tender anterior cervical											
	adenopathy clear											Call if not imp next wk
												WF
8-1-78	cc: Sore Throat 2 day headache											
56#	S- in last 2D started with xonset of sore throat,										Tonsillitis	Penicillin V
T·100	H/A, gen. malaise, some fever as well.										Motion Sickness	Recommended R 1 AM, sample given
	xx Mother also mentions had problems with motion											
	sickness. Particularly troublesome with riding											
	school bus. Has used dramamine as OTC but finds											BH
	that doesn't work well in dose that doesn't promote											
	drowsiness											
	O - X - TM's clear, nose clear but throat reveals											
	tonsillar enlargement, erythema and exudate, submandibular											
	tender adenoapthy											
	supple		N	N	N							
9-19-78	cc: T 104-103° for 2-3 days											
51½#	sore throat - tops of gums red											
T·100.8°	been taking aspirin - stomach aches											
	S - Mother has belated that over the past 48 hrs.										Recurrent tonsilitis	Pen VK 250, 1
	she has had temps. from 102-104 with increased											Fluids, rest,
	soreness of throat. Also Cx of her glands being											Throat cultur
	swollen, gen. H/A. DC activity. Relates to no											Will call res
	ear congest., no cough, gen. feeling of tiredness.											throat cultur
												morrow.
	O - Does not appear acutely ill.											
	Bilat. TM's clear and intact. Nasal passages											
	clear. Oral mucosa, the gums are somewhat redened											
	but no real hypertrophy noted. There is about 2+											
	tonsilar enlargement with erythema and extreme											
	or yellowish exudate. There is anterior cervical											
	node lymphadenopathy which is tender.											
			N	N	N					Skin		
	warm and dry with good color.											
												CT

Gregory, Julie   #179818   DATE OF BIRTH 5-16-69

EYE 1	ENT 2	NECK 3	CHEST 4	HEART 5	ABD 6	G.U. 7	MUSC SKEL 8	NERV 9	SKIN 10	ASSESSMENT	PLAN

CSR 11 mg/hr.

S - Mother relates that over past several wks. she
has been Cx of intermittent sore throat. Appetite
has still not been good but has been common over the
past few yrs. Over the past 48 hrs. has been Cx
of the throat becoming more sore, glands slightly
swollen and been Cx of H/A almost daily. Had a
recent opthalmology exam in which her glasses seemed
to be the right prescription and was advised to cont.
wearing them. Also, relates to some Sx of tiredness.
Has had no nausea, vomiting or diarrhea but been Cx
of some generalized abd. discomfort. She has been
running a low grade temp. over the past wk. never
being more than 99.4 - 99.6.

O - Does not appear in any acute distress.
       Bilat/ TM's clear and intact. Nasal pass.
clear. There is no rhinorrea. There again is about
a 1+ tonsilar enlarg. with extreme erythema and some
patchy yellow exudate bilat. There is some very
small ant. cerv. node lymphadenopathy which is non-
tender.
           GROM, no rigidity.
               Clear to A & P. Good vessicular
sounds. Good expansion.
                   Reg. sinus rhythm. Rate approx.
88.
                   Soft, no palpable
organomegly or tenderness.   Without rashes. Warm and color 7s good. Good skin targer.

Assessment:
Prob. recurrant
mild tonsilitis.

R/O mono.

R/O any rheumatic
fever.

Plan:
CSR 11 mg/hr.
Monospot, CBC, sed
rat, throat cultur
20 min./hr.
Pen VK 250, 1 qid

Fluids, ASA.

Will consult with
Dr. H. after result
come back.

78 cancelled   CT

78 PC: School called - sent her
home today (had appt. for 12/22)
nauseated pale green" T 100°
last aspirin 10:45 AM - throat still
sore - off Pen VK for 3 days only
Seems daily headaches - takes ASA
daily.

78 Pen VK 250 mg x 10 days DW/BH

S - Today a Hx of almost daily problems with H/A's,
nausea, abd. pain, vomiting, fever of 99-100 range
and sore throats, have been present for almost 2
yrs. - seemingly from the time of an A/A in Nov.
1976. Says that she will get Sx's for a day or 2,
then seem better, then come down with them time and
time again. Does not generally bring her in for this
because it always seems to get better.   CONT:

"Well, I've caught it up at a hundred and one, but it seems to be low grade all the time and she has these, oh, I don't know what you'd call them, headaches, I guess, don't you, Julie?" She glances over, I nod. "Tell the doctor about your headaches."

"Do they seem related to any foods she's eating, Ms. Gregory?"

"You can call me Sandy, Dr. Phillips. Well, I try to get her to eat but she's so finicky that she hardly eats a thing since we put her on the allergy diet. And when she does eat, she's nauseated."

"Is the nausea with the headaches?"

"I don't know. Julie, is the nausea with the headache?" Mom flits back to me, pivoting her head on the *L* of her thumb and index finger. At the doctor's she sits up exact and straight and anchors her head into the *L* so that nobody sees her occasional nervous head spasms.

"Is the headache across your forehead, like this," he stretches his face like Silly Putty toward his ears, "or," squishing his hands together, "around your skull like this?"

I look between both of them. What is a headache, *exactly*? Is it when my eyes hurt? Is it when I'm dizzy on the bus? I'm trying to guess, hoping it's the right answer.

"I'm not really sure."

"What do you mean you don't know, Julie?" Mom lashes her head around and contracts her eyes to slits. I swallow. Seconds dangle. I cannot pull away. I'm as glued to her eyes as if my arms were pinned. A crack in the air breaks the spell as she slaps her leg and turns in disgust, "Jesus, Julie, we've been seeing you sick and you've been telling me you've had headaches in the car

all this week. Remember when you've been carsick?"
She turns back to Dr. Phillips. "I'm sorry, Doctor, I don't
know what's wrong with her that she's doing this to me.
There's got to be something wrong with a kid that
doesn't even remember how sick she was just yesterday.
Julie, stop wasting the man's time and tell him what's
going on with you. Now I mean it."

"They're around my forehead like the first one you
said."

Dr. Phillips picks right back up.

"Is it a tight band that squeezes or more of a dull,
throbbing, indirect pain?"

"Uh. A tight band."

"That sounds like it could be a migraine. Why don't
we start her out on a sample of Ergostat, Sandy, and you
can get back to me next week on how this works out."

"Thank you so much, Doctor."

AND WHEN MOM SAYS I don't have a headache, I ride
my bicycle to the next road over, and curve back its
empty lane, pedaling fast along the smooth winding
river of blacktop that loops back onto itself in a cul-de-
sac overgrown with Queen Anne's lace and lofty weeds.
My handlebar tassels whiz in the wind and the colorful
spoke tire pegs blur on my speed machine. My
Honeycomb license plate flaps wildly with each pump of
my legs straddled along a glitter sparkle banana seat.
My long blond hair cascades down my back and I swing
it back and forth in the breeze, swerving all over the
road singing, "*I can't smile without my mom, can't
laugh without my mom.*"

Mom's elbows looked like they were full of buckshot, or wheel bearings. I used to sit in the backseat and hook my armpits over the front so I could slide the loose flesh between my fingers, transfixed by the purplish grainy pebbles moving back and forth under her skin. When I asked her how come she had rocks in her arms, she told me that Grandma Madge had sent her out one night with a carload of boys and she had to jump out the window as they sped onto the highway. The impact of her skid lodged pebbles so far under her skin that they stuck there permanently.

"Why did you jump out the window, Mom?"

"Because I had to, Julie."

"But why?"

"I'll tell you sometime when you're older." And she turns away, lips trembling.

Dad snaps on the radio and leans toward his window. I keep rolling the elbow flap between my fingers, isolating each blue-black pebble to study it closer, watching her tears fall and saying, "I'm sorry, Mommy, I'm sorry you're sad today." But still I keep on rolling.

Another week has gone by and nothing has changed. I still pee the bed and wake up in the morning soaked all the way down to my knees, my sheets and pajamas sticky and stinking. It started when we moved here. I can't help it. And I can't stop.

Mom and I sit in the Township office waiting for Dr. Phillips and I scour the reception room for all the *Reader's Digest*s. I speed-read the short stories and little funnies at the end of each article: "Laughter, the Best Medicine," "Life in These United States," "Humor in Uniform." I hope I can distract Mom into forgetting about the wet clothes she peeled off me this morning. I'd die if my doctor asked me why I wet the bed when I'm seven.

"You know, Mommy, my headaches I think might be worse. This girl at school got glasses and she never got headaches."

"Really, Sis? You noticing them getting worse?" Mom doesn't look up from her *Ladies' Home Journal*. "Well, let's make sure we tell that to the doctor. Good job on thinking about what might be wrong with you."

In the examining room, Mom says, "Now, we're going to tell Dr. Phillips about the dull pains in your head, right about," she presses her fingers into my skull, trying to find them, "here." She squeezes hard to remind me what they feel like.

"Now I don't want any kind of fiasco like we had last time, okay?"

"Okay."

"I'm the mom: I know what's going on here. So if he asks you questions, you just let me answer."

Dr. Phillips breezes in and apologizes for our wait. Mom gives him an update on my allergy diet and pulls out her list of new symptoms. Some he writes down, some he just listens to, moving his eyes between her and his chart. I sit in my sick pose, pretty sure that Mom's forgotten the wet bed.

As she runs down the symptoms, I know some of them aren't all the way true. I sit on the edge of the exam table, my eyes fixed on my knees, but I feel the words rise into my throat, words to correct her, flooding my mouth, rushing to get out. They crash against one another and then pile into a dam of all the words I cannot say. I have to press my tongue to the roof of my mouth to hold them back. Little clucks and ticks swirl around the inside of my mouth and escape through my hanging bottom lip.

Cluck. No, I don't have a sore throat *every day,* just yesterday. *Tick.* No, my fever last night wasn't *way up to 102.*

Cluck, Cluck! No, I don't go to the school nurse *every single* day. Dr. Phillips pauses, his pen lifted mid-sentence.

"Are you okay, Julie?"

I nod up and down.

"See what I mean, Doctor? Something is going on here." When Dr. Phillips steps out to get us a sample of another trial medicine, Mom gives a Spock pinch to my knee and growls I had better knock it off.

A FTER WE'D MOVED BACK FROM Arizona and settled into the white two-story, we'd all driven up to Columbus to see my grandpa—Dad's dad—for the first time since I'd been born. I was thrilled; I'd never met a grandpa from Mom's side, and the great-grandpa who used to write me love letters addressed to "Jewel" had passed away before I could gurgle his name. Mom told me he'd come to the hospital to pick her up when we were ready to go home, but at the last minute, he made Mom drive so he could wind his long arms around me and hold me close. He said I was the most beautiful baby, an elfin queen, a princess, a jewel. The stories I heard about his love for me made him the man I was always waiting to meet again; the first man that got away. Dad didn't want me around Grandma Madge, and his mom had died before I was born, so Chester was my last shot at having a grandparent.

When we pulled up to the VA housing complex where Chester lived, the place seemed deserted.

Mom crossed her arms and said, "I'm going to wait in the car, Dan. Don't be too long."

Dad hadn't seen Chester since he left home for the Navy at sixteen, and I was nervous, too. I was getting a new grandpa today.

Dad and I stood at the curb. He took a deep breath; so did I. We looked at each other, then clasped hands and walked up the sidewalk, scanning the house for signs of life. The curtains were yellowing at the top and streaked with black soot from cigarette smoke; mail sprouted out of the letter box and weathered flyers stuck to the screen door and under the rubber mat in layers. But when we knocked, a gravelly voice warbled out, "Door's open."

We stopped in the hallway, blinded by white spots left over from the July sun, trying to adjust to the darkness. Chester had stacked cases of Bud Light up to the ceiling to block the light from the single window in the living room. Dad sat down on the ottoman between Chester and the television and I climbed on Dad's knee.

"You can call Chester 'Grandpa,' Sissy. Can't she, Chester?"

Chester nodded. "What's your name again, little girl?"

I pointed my thumb to my chest. "I'm Julie, but Dad calls me Sissy."

Chester talked to us during commercials and leaned around us when his show came back on, even though Dad kept on and on; about Arizona, my school, his job at the base, Mom. Chester grunted a few *uh-huh*s and *oh-yeah?*s before he let out a great hissing sigh and began pumping his thumb up and down on the remote volume, drowning out Dad.

At the next commercial Chester said, "Glad you could make it up, Peggy." Peggy was Dad's sister. I knew he was telling us to get out even though we'd only been there fifteen minutes. Dad just sat there. Tears welled up in his eyes and slipped freely down his face. He dropped his head and stood slowly, and I slid off his knee like I was nothing more than a sheet of paper. I wrapped my stick arms around his waist and hugged as hard as I could, clamping one hand around my other wrist and tugging tight. I was not gonna let him go. He stood there, empty, his muscular limbs pinned to his side by the sheer strength of mine.

"I love you, Daddy."

"I love you too, Sissy."

IT WAS USUALLY AFTER MOM slipped the little white pill under my tongue that my migraines got worse.

"I can tell you've got a headache coming on. Here, open up. Lift your tongue. Gooood."

Sometimes I about threw up. Most times, I just needed to climb back into bed, as the pill sank into a pasty chalk under my tongue; that's how bad the headaches got. I still didn't know if they went across my head or over my face, but they burned my whole head on fire, my scalp felt nauseated, and the bottom of my throat jumped and rushed, like a watchdog snapping the leash.

Mom could never get a job because I was so sick. She never knew when a migraine was going to creep up or a fever soar past a hundred or my throat turn red and swollen with infection and she'd have to drop what she was doing and run me into Township.

During the day she scours and straightens each room in our big house, and on the days she thinks I might be sick, she keeps me home from school to watch me. Sometimes I hear her in the kitchen, laughing out loud. When I pop around the corner and ask what's so funny, she startles and says, "Oh, just thinking about a private funny between me and the nurse."

She puts me in the car one afternoon and says, "We are going to have to do something with that hair."

At the beauty salon, I sit in the swivel chair and she tells the lady with scissors to cut my long hair to an X-Y-Z shag, like the mom on *The Brady Bunch*. The woman looks down at my hair. I've been blond since I was a baby, but Mom says my hair's getting darker as I get older, just like hers did. Pretty soon it's going to be growing in dirty dishwater brown. But today I sit, with seven years of blond hair, silky straight, the ends almost white from the sun.

"Are you sure?" the lady asks.

"Look, I've tried and tried to get her to do something with it but this is what I get, so just cut the damn shag!"

I've never had a haircut before so when the lady turns me around to the mirror I don't even know where my hair went; it flips up to my ears, it's brown all over—not blond like I've always seen myself in the mirror.

"I want my hair back!" I cry.

I look ugly, like a boy, and I know so because even Mom starts laughing when she sees me.

MOM SAYS SHE CAN'T STAND ME, she has had it up to *here,* she can't get any help around here, will you please do something with her, Dan? God, she is driving me crazy.

We're upstairs in my bedroom when Dad eases in the front door. Mom is tearing after me, clawing at my X-Y-Z shag, stinging me with her hitting hands. Dad trudges up the steps. "Hey, now, what's going on up here?" He comes in just in time to see me duck. Mom's back is to the door, her wild hair stuck to her face with spit and sweat.

"Sandy, what the hell are you doing?"

"Goddammit, Dan." She swings around and grabs at the canopy post of my four-poster bed. "This girl will not pick up her room, she will not mind. I can't get any help around here. I've had it, Dan, I mean it. You are never around. I can't take it anymore!"

My father is silent, looking at his shoes, listening. He pads across the carpet and leans against my dresser, pushing up his sleeves. "I'll take it from here, Sandy." He turns his face to me and I think I catch him wink. Mom backs away. He yells softly at first, his eyes twinkling into mine and I stop crying, saved by my father and by the pact he's just made with me: Let's do a show and get her off our backs. But the more Mom inches away, the louder Dad gets, until his twinkle turns to black and I am crying even harder because I have never heard my father yell so loud or look so angry.

Dad hooks his fingers around my wrist and tugs me out. He stops in the doorway where Mom's standing, "Now tell your mother you're sorry."

"I'm sorry, Mom."

"Now tell her you love her."

"I love you, Mom."

"Now go over there and give her a hug."

Mom stands bitter with a clamped jaw, looking away, fat tears rumbling down her cheeks. I wrap my arms around her folded ones and give a little, one-pump squeeze.

Dad says, "You're coming with me today, kid, we're going to get you out of Mommy's hair." And he yanks me down the plush steps, with Mom trailing behind. "You know, I can't take it anymore, Dan. I need help around here, you know?"

And Dad says, "I know, Sandy, I know," and lets the screen door slam behind us.

When we get in the car, Dad peels out, slinging gravel at the fence and scorching tire tracks through the side grass. I brace against the dash and catch a glimpse of Mom, her forehead pressed against the door frame, her fingertips slipping down the screen as she sobs. The car spits out onto the pavement and Dad slams into drive. We burn down the road and he smacks the wheel. "We did it, Sissy, we got out today!" I'm filled with a dizzy ecstasy of forbidden and stolen freedom, as if we have zipped out of Township just as Dr. Phillips was walking in.

But as we drive away, I lean my head to the window and tears slip from my eyes. I can't shake the vision of my mother, trapped in the house behind the heavy-gauge screen door, and us taking the only car. My father is calmer now. He reaches out for me and pat, pats my knee.

"Don't worry, Sissy," he says. "Mom is just in a bad mood because a baby is growing in her belly."

Dad and I spend our stolen Saturday sauntering through the big mall, holding hands. The smacks on my skin are almost faded from memory. I've never spent a whole day with my dad before. We meander by old people nodding off on the benches, we marvel at the indoor palm trees and stand in the mist of the thundering water fountains, tossing pennies. Dad dares me to reach in there and grab a few quarters for the candy machines. I don't even care about going to a toy store: I just want to be with my dad.

Somewhere behind us an eruption of laughter ignites and echoes through the four-level chamber of the mall. Dad jumps and spins around to face the sound, terror sweeping across his face. The roar is from a group of friends standing in front of a store, and I laugh, too, because it sure must be funny, whatever it is. Dad looks down at me, ominous. "Sissy, honey, do you know why those people back there are laughing?"

I shake my head.

"They're laughing," he scoops my chin into his giant palm and lifts my face to his, "and I know this is gonna hurt, honey, but they're laughing because of your ugly hair. You're just not pretty like other little girls. I know you're not smart enough to understand that, but I'm your daddy, I'll protect you. Julie, people will screw you with your pants on. But don't you worry, baby girl, stick with me and I'll take care of you."

I look back at the people who laughed at me and they're not even looking at me now, just standing in a little circle facing each other, and I see how sneaky they can be to turn away so fast when they know you're going to catch them making fun of you. Dad starts strolling again and I keep looking back over my shoulder, trying to catch them in the act.

"Love you, Sissy." Dad gives my tiny hand a squeeze in his big one.

"Love you, too, Dad."

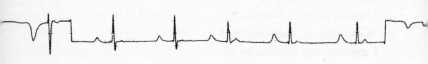

THE DAY MY BROTHER WAS BORN I hopped on the school bus shouting at the driver, "I just had a baby, I just had a baby!"

Daniel Joseph Gregory the Second—complete with a Roman numeral to sound like royalty—weighed in at a whopping ten pounds and was so healthy he had to be cut right out of Mom. Little Danny Joe looked just like a Butterball turkey and, unlike me, he came with a full head of hair and a healthy scream.

Danny was unexpected—a surprise or a mistake, depending on whether you talked to Mom or Dad—but nonetheless a miracle baby since the last two had died before they ever made it out of the hospital.

Dad sings out, "Joe, Joe, broke his toe, riding on a buff-a-lo," beaming over his boy whose name is in the song he loves.

Now that Danny's here, people we don't even know stop by our house to see the baby. Twice-removed relatives send us invitations to family reunions we never knew existed. Even Grandma Madge is talking to Mom about making a pilgrimage from Phoenix to see little Joe, as Dad's started calling him.

Mom coos over his bassinet and says "God love it" whenever Danny does anything from crap a diaper to bounce up and down in his baby bungee jumper, gumming a smile at nothing.

I mimic Mom's words, her voice, her happiness.

"God love it, looook, isn't he just adorable?"

I answer our phone in the same Betty Homemaker voice, picked up from commercials and honed with inflections to match my mother.

"Hello, this is the Gregory residence, how may I help you?"

"Uh, Sandy?"

"Ohhh"(feign surprise). "No, this is Julie, her seven-year-old daughter. If you'll hold just a moment I'll get her for you. May I ask who's calling?"

Mom picks up the line and I hide behind the kitchen partition.

"That's my little helper, God love her."

God did love me and so did my mom. "God love it" may have gone to Danny, but "God love her" went straight to me.

WITH A NEWBORN BABY came all sorts of dangers that threatened my brother's trek from infancy to toddlerhood; frantic ER trips when Mom would find him blue in his crib, an emergency run to the fire department over a possibly poisonous spider bite. But Danny was the cutest and healthiest thing that had ever come out of the Gregory family, and his knack for slipping away from illness and injury was abundant. Dad had the Agent Orange, Mom had the toxemia, Madge was a *battleac,*

Lee was *off,* Chester was brain dead, and I was sickly. But here Danny was: a grinning mound of angelic jiggling baby flesh that knew no bounds of appetite, action, or glee. He was contagious. After Danny, we all felt better, especially me. My migraines just miraculously dried up. I no longer had to stick pills under my tongue, and I even quit peeing the bed. Now that I wasn't sick and staying home from school all the time, I started getting straight A's and reciting Shel Silverstein poems for show-'n'-tell. I was in the top third-grade reading level—reading along with some fourth graders even— and I owed it all to Danny.

Danny became the telescope we looked through from inside our own cloudy bubble, and what we caught was a glimpse of another galaxy, one full of light, laughter, and hope.

ONE DAY AT SCHOOL, I was running on the playground when the whistle blew, and I tripped over somebody's sneaker trying to get into line. I felt my wrist snap as I hit the pavement. I knew it was broken. I didn't cry; I just held it tight to my chest and tugged on the shirt of the recess teacher. She told me I'd have to take it to my teacher. My teacher told me I'd have to take it to the school nurse. And the school nurse called my mother and said she'd have to take it to my doctor.

All afternoon I sit in one of the blue velvet swivel chairs in the good living room as Mom bustles around the house, doing dishes, whistling to the radio, changing Danny. The bone in my arm sticks out a bit through my skin. It throbs now and hot tears flow down my face to match the heat pulsing in my wrist. I want to see Dr. Phillips. I want him to fix it. But Mom says it's probably just a sprain.

"It's just too soon to tell, honey. Let's wait'n' see if the swelling goes down. Mommy's busy here. I got to get supper started before your dad gets home. I'll decide if I should run you in."

It is almost five when Mom calls Township to ask if she should have this little thing seen or hold off another day.

Dr. Phillips shows Mom the X ray, my wrist cracked in three places.

"Hmm, well, I'll be," she says.

It's a good thing she brought me in when she did, he says. Any longer and my wrist wouldn't have set right. Anything like this happens again, don't wait, Sandy, bring her straight in.

When he walks out to get the casting material, Mom whips her face around, "Don't you look at me like that, it could have been just a sprain."

When I fall again in fourth grade, I know my other wrist is broken even before I hit the sidewalk. But Mom says I'm just going to have to wait for my father to get home, it's time he carried his weight around here and took me in to the doctor's for once.

WHERE DAD HAD BEEN when I broke my arm was down in the country, looking for a new place for us to live. He didn't like the eyes of prying neighbors watching us from behind closed curtains, or the church pastors who drove past our house real slow, trying to guilt us into church every Sunday. Dad wanted to get us away from all the crazies out there and especially from the black people who stood around street corners and gas station parking lots. He was sure they were just waiting for the right chance to kidnap one of us and sell us into a child porno ring.

As long as we were home or on a direct route to the medical center, we did all right. But driving into downtown Columbus for Dad's VA appointments, Mom and Dad would turn jittery and wide-eyed.

"Oh, my God, Dan, look at that one over on the corner. Make the light, make it."

Dad flashes his face back to me in the rearview mirror. "Julie, get your door locked. Roll up your window." He sneaks a look over to the black man, who's waiting to cross the street, a comb stuck upright in his great shock of hair. "Fast, get it up, Julie! Sandy, lock your door. Get your purse under the seat."

"Oh, shit, Dan, the light's turning. Don't stop, Dan, don't stop!"

Mom is frantically trying to stuff a purse the size of a bowling ball under the seat and I am furiously cranking the backseat windows up while Dad pops the locks down, then repops them up and down, harder, just to make sure.

The man flows over the curb and down into the crosswalk, his loose undone gait bringing him close to our car, like a real-life safari lion. And there we are, sticking out into the intersection, holding our breath while the man looks at us like we're crazy.

As he passes, Dad guns it and we squeal away.

"Jesus, that was close," Mom says.

Dad's massive forehead fills the rearview mirror, shiny sweat on his brow. "If one of them ever comes up to you kids, I don't care where you are or who you're with, you start screaming at the top of your lungs. You got me?"

"Yeess, Daad."

IT WAS EASTER SUNDAY when I sat for the second time in the blue swivel chair clutching a snapped wrist. When Dad walked through the door later that night, he shouted, "I've found it, the perfect secluded place. Kids, honey, we're getting out of this goddamned suburb and away from the crazies. We're going to the country!"

WE ARE ALL LOADED UP in the long, wide family wagon. Me, three-year-old Danny, porky little arms waving from where he is bound into his car seat, Dad driving and Mom gazing out the passenger window at the fields whizzing by.

The air is hot, even at fifty-five miles per hour. It's like a blanket of oven heat, blasting through the car windows. No more cars to play headlight pididdle with, just open spaces, winding roads, and isolated woods that stand empty by the road, with the occasional cemetery marked only by little white stubby graves popping out of the earth, worn smooth like half-dissolved peppermint Life Savers.

A bee gets blown in the window and lands on my sun-warmed cast, which I take as a compliment. I let him crawl around the plaster and he walks up to where the living skin that sees the sun meets the flakey skin that stays in the dark and dips down into the space my shrunken arm has made at the top of my cast. His feelers rove over my moist arm until I've got a tickle deep in my cast I know I can't reach. I bang on the plaster and spook him out of it. The last thing I need is a sting halfway down my cast.

We pull onto a narrow gravel track off the main paved road. It's single lane and goes down, down, deep into a tunnel of lush green treetops that interlace in a fingery canopy overhead. The car bump-bumps over the washboard rivets etched by years of wheels that have sped up the steep hill like it was their own 4X4 trail. At the bottom, the road pans out into a wider stretch that straightens and exits the woods into thick fields where the weeds grow as high as the car window. We pass a murky shaded swamp, a dilapidated log cabin, and finally—around one more bend—arrive at the grass-covered spot about half the size of a baseball field that will be the site of our new home.

It is desolate. My stomach sinks. The ill-timed siren of a locust goes off in the distance. *Wow, it sure is far out. There aren't any neighbor kids. School must be miles and miles away.*

"We're here." Mom pops her gum, punctuating the silence. "I'm going to call it 'Hideaway Farm.'"

I'm wondering why Mom said this would be such a great place for me, but as soon as little Danny is lifted from his car seat, he drops his pants and squats to pee right there out in the open. We laugh. Then he races all around, like a puppy off his leash, no black people to abduct him, no cars to run him over, and a whole sea of emerald grass to lope through. If Danny's happy, so are we. He's the barometer by which we gauge what's okay for our family and what isn't.

Mom walks over to the only standing building, which

sits on the edge of a hill by the road. It's our very own log cabin straight off the pancake syrup bottle, except the white stuff is caked sloppily between the railroad ties like someone didn't care how it looked. From here, you can almost see the other log cabin we passed across the field. Mom tells me ours is the old original homestead, and that when Mr. Burns built here back in the twenties, he brought along the fortune he'd made robbing banks and sunk it deep into these hills. He named the road after himself and when he died, people came from miles around to dig for his treasure but it never was found.

I make my way out behind the cabin to where the hill drops sharply down. As far as I can see are rusty refrigerators, old stoves, jagged edges of washers, toothy sheets of tin, and heaps of tires, wavy heat rising from the black rubber piled right out there in the blazing sun.

WHEN WE COME DOWN THE ROAD the next time, there is a trailer sitting on the other side of the old cabin and looking out over the hill below. I'm not supposed to hate our new place, but it's nothing like our white two-story with the baby-blue carpet. I try to get excited about my mother's plans for building on a deck here, then one off the back, an extra bedroom, a whole new addition, but why does she keep calling it a house when it's really a tin box that doesn't even have real windows, just little squares of plastic that you have to crank open with a handle? It's a double-wide, she says, the same dimensions as a real house, there's no difference, absolutely none. She calls the place a "farm" too, but it really isn't a farm because we don't have any animals. Even I know a trailer isn't a house and a dump isn't a farm, but this is our Hideaway and we're here just in time for the summer.

THE MINUTE WE MOVED IN, Dad wanted to start building a GTO, his vision of the ultimate oldies cruising machine. He picked up local *Tradin' Times* papers and *Pontiac* newsletters and started stockpiling junk parts around the trailer; slightly bent bumpers, old exhaust manifolds, random door panels, and rust-crusted windshield wiper motors. The parts stayed half wrapped in the newspaper they were shipped in (the better ones stashed on his closet shelf, the big ones slid under the trailer), until he could build himself a garage off the side of the log cabin. But Mom had different plans for him. She wanted Dad's free time devoted to building onto the house. She wanted him in a backhoe, digging us out a pond over the hill. She wanted that deck off the back and a bigger dining room for holiday dinners and parties with relatives and friends, her eyes literally glowing with plans for the future. And Dad was always in the awkward position of trying to prove to her that he was the man of the house.

The whole time we were growing up Mom told us a story behind Dad's back whenever they were fighting and she wanted us to side with her. We still don't know if there was any truth to it, but as kids, we hung on every word and swallowed this dark family secret, and the shame that went with it. Supposedly, back in the seventies when I was just a baby, Dad took on a lover. But that wasn't even the worst of it. According to the story Mom spit out through clenched teeth, Dad's lover was a guy.

"The faggot. Your father, nothing but a good-for-nothing, lazy-assed faggot."

So Dad's manhood became an overstatement he needed to make—as much to reassure himself, as for the sake of self-protection. An overstatement that spawned piles of greasy-cornered *Ohio Swinger* magazines of spread-eagle locals stacked up under his workbench, and that prompted him to comment on every overt physical attribute of any female who walked by. Otherwise, all Mom needed to do was drop a few choice words.

And what Mom wanted for herself was to have a bunch of horses and her kids in 4-H, reciting the youth group's pledge, hand over heart:

> *I pledge*
> *My head to clearer thinking,*
> *My heart to greater loyalty,*
> *My hands to larger service, and*
> *My health to better living,*
> *For my club, my community, my country, and*
> *   my world.*

She wanted to stick us in horse shows, she wanted us wearing ten-gallon hats and silver conchs sewn down our thrift store polyester trousers, winning ribbons like she always wanted as a kid. And as soon as I got my cast off, there we were in August, at the United Methodist Fun-raiser horse show, sweltering in the back of the horse trailer, peeling off our show ring outfits and soaking in our resentments for getting dressed up like her personal cowboy dolls.

And all Danny and I really wanted to do was lounge through the summer and play in the aboveground pool we bought secondhand out of the paper. But Mom had to have barbwire strung up and hay baled and half-starved horses from the livestock auctions, that would have gone to slaughter if she hadn't stepped in to outbid the meat buyers by a few measly dollars.

We worked like slaves trying to get it all done. The pool sat empty but for a few bright green tree frogs under the slimy liner and a rippling surface full of stranded June bugs. The heavy-gauge barbwire fought us tooth and nail and clung to the spool like barnacles on a rib cage. Mom and I ran it for miles, up hills and through briar patches, stapled it into leaning trees and wrestled it around ancient rotting fence posts, stretching it taut until my hands bled. And as soon as we got one thing done, there was always something else pressing to do before we could be happy or relax. By the time Danny was four he could teeter a sheet of drywall on his head while I fed the tall end to Dad to hammer onto the studs. Even little Danny, who used to smile incessantly, started walking around worried that Mom would catch him playing and get the flyswatter.

There weren't enough hours in the day to do extraneous chores like brushing our teeth, or—once we started school—homework. Sometimes Mom'd scrape her fingernail up and down on one of our front teeth and get a rind of yellowy paste under her nail. "I see you got some sweaters building up on your snags," she'd say. "You better get in there and brush."

In the mornings, we scraped our sweaters off over bowls of sugary cereal, heaped high with tablespoons of more white sugar until there was a thick crusty layer on top. At night, we'd fall asleep exhausted and sweaty, like sticky glazed donuts. Come the next day, we'd start all over again.

And if Mom didn't stay on top of Dad, he'd drop

what he was doing the minute the coast was clear and plop down in his chair.

When Dad settles in, he dominates the television and therefore any room that borders the living room. If you coast along on the couch with his daily ride of TV, you'll find yourself making several dozen trips to the kitchen for a diet pop, jelly toast, or any other snack he hankers for. Since we moved down here, Dad's belly has started to get huge, even though he drinks a six-pack of Tab every day. If the batteries run down on the remote, he'll make you perch under the console and click through the channels as his living remote. Once cemented in his chair, Dad'll hawk into his hand and fling it against the wall or the carpet. But if he knows you're anywhere near, you'll have to fetch him toilet paper and haul it off, clamping the dry edge of the damp wonton pouch daintily between two fingers. If you can, it's best to slip into your room when no one's looking.

And in my room, there are stacks of books—from Christmas, from the library, swiped from waiting rooms. I read them over and over, climbing into bed on perfectly sunny days whenever I can sneak away to hide between the pages of my favorite escape.

OVER THE YEARS, OUR LITTLE TRAILER would grow into a labyrinth, with bedrooms and baths and living rooms, and even separate quarters for the veterans and foster kids Mom brought to the farm, all tacked on to one another and sprouting out from every side. We were surrounded by a moat of thick, lush, woods; a protective screen that kept us in a hidden world, our isolated bubble at the bottom of that hollow; our own private ecosystem brewing in a self-imposed petri dish.

But at the top of the road, we rose to the occasion: Town. Everybody looked presentable before we left the house. That meant color-coordinated outfits for me, Garanimals for Danny, and clean underwear on us both. That meant Danny's sun-blond hair was combed to the side and sprayed stiff and mine was curl-ironed for body and then feathered flawlessly with the thick Goody comb Mom made me carry in my purse for touch-ups. We clicked into our seat belts and straightened our spines. We rolled out from under the cover of a thousand trees and the radio came alive, the gray crackling of a station without a signal suddenly turning to song. We might have to pause at the top of our dirt road for another car to pass by on the paved one, but when they did, we casually peered into their car windows and we looked *just like them*! And then we merged. Into the road, on toward civilization, past real houses with neighbors who knew each other, past suburbs like the one where we used to live and into crowded Kmarts and busy waiting rooms with people from all walks of life.

Because ultimately, what came down to being the only thing important enough to break us from the work or jeopardize our safety, was starting back up with my doctor to find out what was wrong with me.

WHEN FIFTH GRADE BEGINS at my new school, Mom works it out with my principal so she can take me out of class if she gets a last-minute doctor appointment. When he announces over the homeroom speaker: *Julie Gregory to the principal's office, please. Your mother is here,* I know to gather up my stuff for the day and race up the steps to meet Mom, because we won't be coming back.

Dr. Phillips prescribes us more migraine medicine and gives us the names of specialists who can see me for the rest of my symptoms. But Dr. Phillips is getting old. He stands against his counter and doesn't even write down the things Mom tells him anymore. He starts calling Mom Ms. Gregory instead of Sandy like he used to, even though she keeps asking him to call her by her first name. He tells us we should get a different primary-care physician, somebody who can handle a case that's as complicated as mine's getting. And then he leaves. He just walks right out before Mom is even done running down the list she brought.

"I can't believe that. Did you see him, Julie? He just walked out on us! Well, if he's going to treat me like that, *Jesus!*"

"Don't worry, Mom, we'll just go find another one."

"That's right, if he's going to pull that shit, we'll show him, we'll just go someplace else."

And we did. Sometimes clear over to other counties to try out new doctors who would do the tests Mom was starting to read about in waiting rooms. And sometimes we even venture up to Columbus, cruising the sea of anonymous two-story brick medical buildings, with their promising specialist signs and insurance-accepted window stickers of hope. It's okay as long as we can stay on the outskirts and avoid having to pop our door locks down.

Mom rails behind the wheel, "How dare he? Call me Ms. Gregory! Tell us to go someplace else! And I'm dragging myself around all because of you!"

When Mom spots a promising sign she huffs, "Jot that number down so we can give them a call back at the house."

I scan the streets, pen to paper, desperate to spot the right one that will calm my mother down. "That one looks like they'd be good, I'll get the number. Okay? *Mommy?*"

"Jesus, Julie, you don't have to ask. Why don't you take initiative and help me out for once? Do I have to do everything around here?"

At night, Dad occupies the living room until the news at 11 is over, then Mom takes over, curling up on the far end of the velour sofa, under the single floor lamp that casts a halo of light around her body. She's perfectly still, buried in a book, with her grocery store reading glasses hanging on to the tip of her nose.

I pad out to the kitchen for water in the middle of the night and Mom is still up, licking her fingers and cornering through the pages of the thick *Medical Journal for Home Use Manual*.

"Whatcha doing, Mommy?"

"Oh," she says, distracted, "just looking, Sis."

"For what?"

"Well, you're sick again, hon, and this book is helping Mommy figure out what's wrong with you."

"Is anything bad wrong with me?"

"You got a lot of the symptoms in here, babe, but there's all kinds of tests that'll help us rule out some of the more serious diseases. We got a list of doctors here so we're in good hands, 'kay, Sissy?"

"Nkay. Good night, Mommy."

"Good night, sweetie."

A NOTHER GRUELING SUMMER NIGHT, with the day spent laying drywall and stringing barbwire. Mom was serving up steaming pot roast from the crock pot. She'd stuck it in that morning, we worked all day, and here we were filthy and sweat-stained, having wandered like battered and confused moths to the warm glow of the kitchen screen door.

Dad stood hunched, catching his breath, gripping the back of a yellow dinette chair, his wife-beater tank covered in lawn clippings, his leg hairs coated green from grass juice as he'd run along the walkways and trailer edges trying to get it all Weedwacked before dark.

Mom was clanging plates down on the table. "Dan, I mean it, we had better get something else lined up here. We need to get that back bedroom done and the deck on before winter."

Mom was pushing to get a license to take care of old men left over from the Second World War because rumors were flying that the base was going to close down next year. And Mom still couldn't take on outside work. My migraines had come back and I seemed to always be tired and carsick. And Mom'd heard a hiccup in little Danny's chest and had started looking up his symptoms at night, along with mine.

"Look, Dan, I got two sick kids on my hands here and there's no way I'm going to take some minimum wage job while you sit on your ass and watch *M*A*S*H* all day."

Having vets, Mom argued, was the only way we could double our income to prepare for Dad getting laid off, keep on building, and still let her be the mom.

"Besides," she added, "Chester was such a lousy

son-of-a-bitchin' excuse for a grandfather that it'll be like having a bunch of nice old grandads. Wouldn't you like that, kids?"

"Yeess, Mom," we droned.

"Why don't you tell that to your father, then?"

"Sandy," Dad said from right next to us, "I don't think these kids oughta be around old men like that. You don't know what could happen, it just ain't worth the money."

"But Dan, if you don't—"

"Goddammit, woman, that's enough! I'm not going to talk about it anymore. Now let's eat!"

And we all sat down for dinner, cautiously sliding our hands out on the table into one another's palms while Dad bowed his head and said grace.

We ate in silence. Danny and I tuned to our plates and set our plastic tumblers on the table without so much as a whisper of sound, while with each clank of Dollar-Mart silverware Mom and Dad jockeyed for touché in a nonverbal fencing match.

Mom turned to me, a high bird caught in her throat. "Are you done? Is that all you're going to eat? I mean, why the fuck do I even cook around here, if you're not going to eat it?

"Dan?"

"Huh?" Dad said, his mouth full.

"Dan, did you even hear me? I said look at what this girl's eating over here. Are you going to get involved here and be a man or do I have to do everything around here? *Jeeesus Christ.*"

"Julie, eat your meat for your mother."

"Oh, is that it? *Chewely, eat yor meat for yor muther.* Yeah, like that really carries the weight of a man. You fairy-assed faggot, you goddamned good-for-nothing son of a bitch."

Dad bangs his knife down. "Dammit, Julie, eat your goddamned meat. Now eat it before I make you eat it."

"Dad, it's gristle." I was sliding it around my plate, trying to tuck it under the mashed potatoes.

"Dan, I've had it with you. You can't even make a little girl mind. You can't even get respect from a sickly little girl. Why do you think she's sick all the time? Why do you think she can't keep up with the work around here? *Huuuh?* Because nobody takes any authority around here to make the kid eat. And you're just going to sit there like Chester," she twiddles her thumbs together, "'Okay, um, now, um, why don't you eat your meat, honey.' You make me sick. You are such a poor excuse for a father. How do you think you're ever going to be a man when you can't even support your own family or make this girl mind?"

Dad slams down his fist and the silverware trampolines up from the table. "Goddammit, Julie, it's just fat, it'll put meat on your bones." He springs from his chair. "I said eat it!"

Before I know it, he's behind me. My head flies back and lands in his massive palm, as he stuffs the greasy rind into my mouth, "I said eat it, girl."

My mother is watching, fork hung in midair, flakey pot roast dangling. Danny is staring at his own roast; soundless tears, held breath.

"I told you, you better listen to your father, but nooooo, you don't think he's a man, do you? You think he's a wimp and you can just walk all over him, huh? Yeah, that's what you think he is, nothing but a sorry-ass, faggot-assed bastard."

Dad's fingers are prying around my mouth, his huge hands fingering a lunk of gristle to the back of my throat, like the Jolly Green Giant trying to stuff a thread through a needle eye of flesh. My eyes water; I gag. By the time he gets back to his chair, I've thrown up the string of fat, along with a whole pile of other stuff.

"Well, at least she ate it, Sandy. I'll have no child of mine disobeying me under my roof." He shakes his fork at me. "You got that, young lady? I'm King in this house."

Mom had the most beautiful singing voice. We'd be in the car on the way to the doctor and Mom would start singing, "*Dust on the Bible. Dust on God's Holy Word. The words of all the prophets and the saviors of our Loorrd. When all the other books are gone, there's none shall make you whole. Get that dust off that Bi-ble and redeem your poor soul.*"

She'd sing about an old Indian named Kawliga, with a heart made of knotty pine, who fell in love with the Indian maiden down at the cigar store. She wore her beads and braids and hoped someday he'd talk. One day a wealthy collector came along, scooped her up and once hidden away, she was never seen again. Even then, I knew Mom was the maiden.

"*Poor old Kawliga, he never got a kiss, poor old Kawliga, he don't know what he missed. Is there any wonder, that his face is red, Kawliga the poor old wooden head.*"

There was Boxcar Willie, too, and the song Mom

sang most every time we took the hour-long drive to a medical center. *"Can you hear that lonesome whippoor-will? He sounds too blue to fly. The midnight train is com-in' home, I'm so lonesome IIIII coouuld die."*

Sometimes Mom cries when she sings. Her voice doesn't break stride for an instant but her cheeks get shiny rivers running down. I tell her she sings so good she should be on the radio.

"Aw, Sis, who'd ever pay to listen to my warbling voice?"

"I would, Mommy! I'd pay a million dollars to have you sing for me! You sound just like Patsy Cline on the radio."

When Dad's driving, he turns up the volume on the dial or says, "Sandy, Jesus, will you sing to yourself, I'm trying to think over here."

But when we're alone, Mom shimmies her back to sit upright, settles her hands on the wheel, lifts her head and opens her mouth to sing so loud it fills the whole car. And I sing right along with her, songs from the days of Smokey and gospel tunes from the one-room country tabernacles we go to sometimes. Mom can yodel from her years traveling around with the Grand Ole Opry, and when she gets going it sounds like there's a yo-yo motoring up and down her throat. I try to yodel with her and even though I don't get beyond the Swiss Miss yodel-lay-he-hoo jingle, there we are, belting out our song, her looking down at me and smiling, and me—fueled by her love—raising my voice to the heavens.

MOM HATED TO SEE any creature go hungry.

"Oh, honey, I can't stand to see that colt starving like that. Poor thing's just penned in there, can't go

anywhere." We passed the same colt with his ribs showing every time we drove to town.

"Julie, get a bucket and put in two scoops of oats
and molasses so we can feed him on our way in."

And Mom was always on the lookout for cruelty to
animals. If we were driving along the highway and there
was a black trash bag puffed up and knotted at the top,
full of trash someone'd thrown out their window, she'd
pull over and have me run out and check to make sure it
wasn't full of kittens. To this day, I still eye roadside
garbage bags, checking for the movement of baby animals trapped inside.

We grew up surrounded by dogs. The manged, matted, starved, and dumped all found their way into our
lives and then down to the farm.

We got Ebony when we first moved in, a black
shaggy farm dog that most all rural properties have at
least one of roaming around. And Mom started to breed
a few purebred dogs she picked up out of the paper, just
to make a few extra bucks, so we have little Pekinese
and Shih Tzus living in pens out by the log cabin. I've
been able to talk Mom into letting me keep my favorite
Shih Tzu, P. J., inside. When she has her puppies, we pen
them up in the laundry room and Mom sells the litter as
soon as she can. P. J. howls and cries for days when
Mom takes her babies away, pacing back and forth, trying to claw over the baby gate to look for them. And
that's when I steal her away and tuck her under the covers with me, holding her tight, helping her forget. I keep
her in my room for weeks at a time, hoping Mom won't
notice, sneaking her outside twice a day and feeding her
canned dog food under my bed.

Our latest addition was a puppy we plucked off the

highway when he was trying to eat something smashed in the road. You could count every link of cartilage in his tail. I hopped out of the car and scooped him up by the scruff of his neck. He rooted through Mom's purse and gulped down a whole pack of Velamints.

"Oh, you stinking pup!" Mom said.

And that's what we called him. Stink Pup.

Our two farm dogs saw me through scary trips out to the garage to turn off the lights for Dad to walking miles of fence lines for Mom in sweltering summer heat. Ebony was easygoing and always seemed to be covered with burrs from running through the woods. Stink Pup was high-strung and as protective of food as we were of our privacy. He had an eagle eye to capitalize on any grub he could lay claim to. We once baited our fishing lines with bacon because I'd snuck out to the worm bucket and set them all free. I hated to fish now: watching Mom thread the worm on the hook and lower him to be eaten alive sometimes made me cry right there on the banks of the pond. So whenever I could, I'd dump the bucket over and blame it on a possum. But the bacon we used instead of live bait didn't work that night. We didn't even get one nibble. We propped our rods against the tack shed and come the next morning, Stink Pup was dragging a fishing pole around the yard, a hook caught through his swollen top lip, bacon fat sewn to his face.

Mom laughed when she saw him, "Go grab the needle-nose pliers, Sis. Stink Pup's taken the bait and got caught; hook, line, and sinker."

SINCE SIXTH GRADE STARTED, I've missed so many days the school sent out a letter saying I'd have to be held back if I didn't get better.

But doctor days are when we get all the shopping out of the way. Otherwise, it's a whole separate trip to town and Mom doesn't like to drive it on her own. And since the day's shot anyway, no harm in stopping in at that new discount clothing outlet that opened up. Might as well kill two birds with one stone.

Mom and I both grab carts and dart through the store, piling anything in that looks worth trying on.

"What'ya think of this, Sis? For the beach?" Mom holds up a gold lamé cruise ship ensemble.

"Oh, I think that'd look great on you, Mom!"

We spend hours in the dressing rooms, hauling armfuls of colorful clothes in front of the three-way mirrors. Mom stands outside my door and says, "How's it going in there, Sis? Let me see when you get it tried on." I take tremendous pride in the fact that I can still wear little girl size 6X.

I open the door and she straightens the pants, smooths the shirt, and tells me yes or no. I toss the nos over the riser and Mom puts them all back on hangers for me. Then I get to do the same when she tries on her brimming cart. Since you're only allowed ten pieces at a time, I run out to the cart again and again to swap out the nos.

We buy sets of different clothes for all the different things we do; clothes for school, clothes for the doctors, clothes for church, clothes for when we get the house done and can start making friends to have down. Then we load the wagon to the brim with fifty-pound bags of horse feed, twenty-five-pound bags of dog nuggets, and sacks of groceries—not to mention new concrete animals from Farm and Fleet for the yard and life-size ceramic dogs and cats, covered in calico fabric and shellacked to a shine, for inside the trailer.

I sit in the front seat and pile the shopping spree bags between my feet on the floor. We're heading back home with new selves; from Penney's Outlet, Sears, Value City, and Kmart. As the sunlight of the city fades behind us, I rummage through the bags, touching the fabric of my new life, *starting as soon as tomorrow,* imagining just how good I'm going to look and how much the kids at school are going to like me now. By the time we hit the stores, I'm so excited about what we're going to get that I don't even remember going to school that morning. And the two hours we just spent at the doctor's has all but drained from my thoughts. Each stop we make perforates my memory just a little more until the page of earlier events is torn away. All that matters is the bag of clothes between my feet, my mother content beside me, and the delicious feeling that everything's going to be better from here on out.

As we pull into Burns Road, Mom says if I don't have time to do my homework tonight I can just do it on the bus tomorrow morning, 'cause by the time I unload the bags of grain, dog food and groceries, feed the horses, and do all the dishes after dinner, it's going to be way past my bedtime.

I AM SUPPOSED TO PEE in this cup. But I can't. I can't tell anybody that I forgot and went already while Mom waited at the reception desk.

I take the cup anyway and sit in the bathroom with the cold little napkin that's folded in a packet, but nothing. I scrape the cup along myself but I can't even squeeze out one little drop. Mom'll be furious. If I can't perform for the doctor, he might not see me. I've got to get us in there. We drove all the way up here. I skipped school to see a new specialist. I have got to do it. I push the cup hard around myself until it leaves an indented ring. Then I turn the cold water on in the sink, and stretch my hand out under it, leaning my forehead on the cold white porcelain. Nothing. I've been in here fifteen minutes, and not one tinkle. I leave the cup on the sink and slink back to the waiting room.

Mom knows. I slip next to her and she sinks her claws into my thigh. She leans over like she's telling me a secret, keeping her face relaxed. She twists a hunk of my leg and breathes mean in my ear. She clamps my elbow between her thumb and forefinger and steers me up to the reception desk.

"Excuse me. Ma'am?" Then she turns to me. "Now, tell her what you did."

"I'm sorry, I couldn't, you know, go."

"That's okay, honey, we'll just reschedule you for another—"

"Look, there has got to be something wrong with this kid, she can't even do one simple test. This has never happened before; she must have something seriously going on here. Can the doctor just please look at her?"

"It's really okay, Ms. Gregory. This happens all the time with children."

"Well, it's never happened with this one!"

"I'm sorry, but the urine sample is a requirement for all new patients."

The nurse reschedules us and I tiptoe away to the woolly fabric chairs of the waiting room. They are so wide three of me could sit next to each other as my feet dangle, swinging above the floor. I scooch over to the far side of the chair and rest my scrawny wrist on the cold metal arm. It's as skinny as the armrest, skinnier even! I pride myself on how little space I take up. I am going to shrink and shrink until I am a dry fall leaf, complete with a translucent spine and brittle veins, blowing away in a stiff wind, up, up, up into a crisp blue sky.

I envision myself growing paper thin. Mom lovingly takes care of me and does everything because I'm a frail but smiling child, riddled with a cancer you can't see. I imagine my beautiful bald head, how cool my silk headscarf will look, knotted at the nape of my pale neck, trailing down my back. I am untouchable. No one ever makes fun of the cancer girl. And everybody is nice to her because they never know when she's going to die.

I DREAM A DREAM THAT NIGHT that stays with me for life. I'm sliding my feet along our slate-bottomed creek, the muddy water rushing around my ankles after a torrent of rain. My mother has always warned me to never walk in the creek after a storm; all it takes is one piece of slate to wash away and you could fall into an underground cavern and be trapped forever. I think of her words as I inch along, clutching for branches and gripping my toes. My heel slips on slick moss, and as I try to catch myself, the slate crumbles under my foot like pie crust. I'm swept off my feet into an underground shaft, angled like a water slide. The walls are smooth wet clay and I slide faster and faster, flying down into the core of the earth on a bed of rushing water. The faster I slide, the narrower, steeper, and drier the tunnel, until I am shooting down a pike, tightening around me, pinning my arms to my sides. I am not scared. I accept the fall. I fall and fall and I know, in my dream, that I will never, ever be able to crawl up the sides and break surface to the light again.

TO _____

PATIENT   Julie Gregory   #1798.18

CC _____

HX: See attached form.
This patient has had documented tonsilitis in August, September
and now persistant troubles in December. There are many other
symptoms the mother relates, some of which are probably totally
unrelated to this. I would appreciate your evaluation of the
throat problem. She did have a normal upper GI in March of this
year.

Other Problems:

Physical Findings:

Lab:

I would appreciate knowing the results of your evaluation. Please
inform me prior to any further referral or hospitalization.

DATE ___ December 20, 1978 ___   SIGNED _____

_____ M.D.

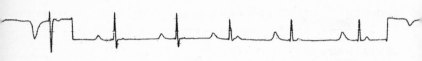

THE FIRST OLD WAR VETERAN to shuffle down our rough gravel walkway and into the trailer was Mr. John Beck. Mr. Beck was a leftover from the Second World War. Most of his life had been spent in a VA hospital. He'd never married and his pension and disability checks stockpiled into an account he didn't have authority to use on his own. If he needed money, he had to ask the person in charge of him and they'd see what they could do.

Mr. Beck would come shuffling down the hall, sliding the plastic feet of his Kmart slippers along the carpet. He'd reach out his thick bruised arms, one after another, for chair backs and counters, the edge of a fish tank, a sort of land-bound trapeze artist trying to make it to the toilet in time.

Beck, as Mom called him, was diabetic. He shot insulin; or rather she shot him with insulin twice a day, sometimes doubling up the doses if she didn't get around to it on his marked schedule.

Beck looked like a weathered eggplant in the markdown produce section. The dark purply tissue under his skin was just as hard as muscle, but discolored and taut, like death was already in there, hardening things up from the inside out. After an endless time in the bathroom, he'd journey back to his bedroom and drop stiffly—his legs, swollen into tree trunks, literally did not bend—into his recliner in front of his tiny black-and-white TV. It got only one channel: fuzzy.

Every day Mr. Beck sat in his chair, snaked his way to the toilet, and shuffled to the kitchen table when Mom called him. He ate before us because Mom couldn't stand the sight of him chewing with his mouth open, a gaping dark toothless hole, bits of food careening down his front.

When the old men first came, Mom would make a nice dinner and we'd put the leaves in the wood-look dining table, drag in some good chairs, and attempt to have a family meal. Mom would cock her head and try to engage the men in conversation, asking about families or what they did in the war, but most of them couldn't hear, or were too drugged up from their government-issue meds to do anything more than nod, their chins inches above their plates. And some of them could hear, but just didn't give a shit to be talking to any of us. They knew we were only nice to them because there was a check attached at the end of the month and they weren't going to extend niceties; we worked for them. It didn't take long before Mom stopped letting them eat with us and called them to the table in mid-afternoon. And soon after that, she stopped making them separate meals, and started giving them slop—our extended-stay leftovers—all mixed together and heated up in one of the old pans with the Teflon flaking off, because she said they couldn't taste anything anyway.

And all the while these men came and went, the

strong ones getting removed, the weak ones slipping into our lair, there sat our constant, Beck, in his flannel shirt and too-short polyester checked pants. In his tube socks with their stretched-out elastic down around his ankles, his legs of wood, his eggplant skin and turtle leathery face.

He stayed with us for years, the best vet of all, riding out the trip to Disney World Mom paid for from his account, sitting in silence for hours, sweltering, parked in the truck with the windows rolled up and the doors locked while we wandered the theme park. And on the days Mom would be gone until dark, taking me to the doctor, she'd lock Beck's door and stick a black plastic garbage bag on the seat of his easy chair.

FROM THE OUTSIDE, my mother personified normal. Unlike her earlier Smokey days, with the fringed leather, yoked western outfits, performer's smile, and platter-sized turquoise belt buckles, her days with my father were dampened to flat. She tucked herself neatly into a smooth, sane parenthesis. Pastel colors, simple blond wigs, an eager, yearning face that cocked just so when she was talking to someone outside our family. She used attentive *uh-huh*s and *I know*s sprinkled like clockwork within a conversation. It was as if every cell in her had mutated and was now divided and eagle-eyed, joining forces to work overtime, straining to connect her to anyone she wanted to impress.

Her head would crane forward to show undying interest in whatever was being said, whether it be the price of pork bellies or the latest politics she didn't have a clue about. She'd nod in agreement, her eyes locked, direct and penetrating, on to the subject before her, her hand in that *L*—thumb under chin, two fingers resting to the side of her face. My mother could have been a model to train stewardesses. Her antennae were so keen that the twitch in a doctor's mouth or the pivot of his turn at the examining table would tell her he was getting ready to dismiss my illness and she'd have to convey to him the urgency of doing one more test, just to be sure his wasn't the key that unlocked the answers. She could sniff out a speck of indifference in the air.

And now that we had Beck and Dad still had his job—not to mention the extra money from selling litters of puppies—Mom had over a hundred pairs of shoes in her bedroom closet. They lined up in tidy color schemes to await the dates, dinners and couples events my father would someday take her to. I used to squat down and count them. It was like a shoe museum. The shoes filled the double closet that ran the length of the master bedroom, and when Dad finished the additional bedroom that made it twice the length, she ran them down the sunken step into the add-on and all the way down the wall to the back of the room. Twenty feet of shoes, three pairs deep: cork wedgies, cowboy boots in every color—some with the high fashion heel for line dancing—classic low pumps, plastic jellies for the beach, rope espadrilles—there they sat, like land mines, ready to detonate whenever she got lost in her closet trying on clothes and realized her youth was rotting away on this Godforsaken appliance pit, with this absentee husband, saddled with these ungrateful kids.

DAD COMES HOME FROM WORK, stands on the tiny looks-like-stone foyer by the door, and singsongs, "Sisssssy, Dannnny," and we come skittering through the hall like hound puppies. I fling into his strong arms, while Danny tries to wrap his little ones around Dad's gargantuan rock-hard middle or just settles onto a single leg. Despite his enormous belly, Dad's still got chicken legs with stick calves and, despite his big Popeye arms, a slender, solid wrist, packed hard with muscle.

After Dad hugs us, he plops down in his recliner, grabs the side handle on his chair for a choppy three position ease back, flicks on *M*A*S*H,* and says, "Fetch me a diet pop, Sissy." Mom waits in the kitchen for him to find her and give her a kiss, which he usually forgets, and she spits out to the living room, "Don't make her wait on you hand and foot, Daaannn," drawing his name out. And Dad shouts back from his chair, "She likes it, don't you, Sissy?" To which I always nod yes because Dad likes me best when I'm fetching for him.

The food Dad consumed collected around his throne like a 7-Eleven altar: pretzel rod bags with salty bottoms and a few split stems, a mound of faded pink pistachio shells, old cups of fizzless Tab, globs of jelly that he'd wiped down the side of the chair. Every week I'd get out the canister vac and suck up the gunk from the deep folds of the furniture, along with whatever Beck had dropped around his place at the table.

But sometimes, if Mom has spent too much time in her closet, she'll have to talk to Dad the second he comes in the door. She even calls him at work and says he had better get straight home here and do something with these kids. They are out of control. She tunes her ears for the sound of his car pulling in at the top of the road and rushes to the living room to wait at the door.

"Dan," she hits him the second he steps in, "you have got to do something with these kids. They are driving me nuts." Dad stands in the foyer, lunch box in hand, blinking out the sun to adjust to the dark trailer. Mom rattles off what we've done that day, things we could never do. We were kids who knew the Lord's Prayer by heart and made burnt matchstick crosses at summer Bible camp. We knew all the Sunday school stories and thought hell was a place you burned for eternity if you didn't finish your meat loaf. And we even spread the gospel to kids at school that the Lord was *our* Savior. Our mouths didn't know how to make the words "bitch" or "cunt," and our heads certainly didn't know what they meant. But that's what Mom says we call her.

Dad just stands there, still in his muddy steel-toed boots.

"What are you going to do about this, huh? These kids need a father that disciplines them, they need to be straightened out."

"What'd ya want me to do, Sandy, beat 'em?" He's tired. "Look at them—they're two beautiful kids who were kids today. You want me to beat 'em for that?" We exhale. Mom amps up the heat, that little white blob of spit starts to flick between her top and bottom lip, she leans toward him, hand thrust on hip.

"Okay." She slaps her leg. "You leave me no choice. I wasn't gonna tell you this, but you have got to know how out of control these damn kids are." Danny and I stand very stiff at the velour couch, whimpering.

She glares at us. "See what I mean, Daaann? They won't even give their own mother respect to talk. And you're just going to stand there and let them walk all over me."

"Kids, let your mother talk."

"Okay, Daaann, let me telllll you what these bastards did. And then you are really going to want to take your belt off and beat the living crap out of them." I pinch a hunk of velour, Danny hops from leg to leg.

"They were out there in your garage today, all right?" Dad perks up. "All right?" she says again, to get his nod. "And when I walked in they were playing in your toolbox." He lifts his head. His toolbox. She gains.

"I told 'em, 'Kids, you know what your father says about you playing with his tools, now you get out of there.' And you know what they said, Dan?"

He wants to know. What did these damn kids say when they were playing with the tools they know better than to be messing with?

"They said, and I kid you not, Dan, they said," her mouth twists, 'Scrreeew him, fuuuccck him.'" Dad is unbuckling his belt.

"Then they said, 'He's crazy, he's too stupid to notice!' And you know what they did? They took your new ratchet and threw it in the pond, while I was screaming after them, begging them to stop!"

We are hanging on every word, eyes like saucers. When she gets to the clincher, Danny and I yelp in protest.

"Are you calling your mother a liar? Huh? Answer me, dammit. Are you trying to tell me your mother would stand here and make things up, lie to my face? I'm your father, how stupid do you think I am? Get your pants down, boy."

Danny has never been hit with a belt before. His

screams crack the air and drown out my own worried cries. Dad hauls back his burly arm and welts raise like oven biscuits on Danny's soft baby skin. For me, it will be different. I'm older. I know better. I unbuckle my pants but I'm too old to be bending over the couch for my father. I grip my fingers onto the fat arm of the sofa but I can't quite make my lower half maneuver over to the leather belt Dad's snapping. His voice bellows over my tiny one, delicate, frantic, trying to explain.

"You got the count of three, girl. One, TWO—" He swipes out for my arm and I break, dashing out the patio screen door, leaping off the deck, running around the pool. He charges after me and catches my weak wrist. I jerk back from my own momentum and he flings me in the grass, flailing the belt over my arms, my legs, my head, my face. I am branded by my father's favorite belt, its leather piping edges raising ruby-tinged bolts on my skin. Mom slips out the front door and creeps to the garage. She's got to get that tool out of the box, just in case he checks.

BUT ON THOSE GOOD DAYS AFTER DINNER, when Mom has slipped into pastels that morning, when she has curl-ironed her hair for an hour and sprayed it luminously with an industrial-size pink metallic can of Aqua Net, when she has selected the precise pair of shoes to wear for my doctor's appointment that day, when she has me watch her get ready and tell her how good she looks, when she tells me to stand on the edge of the tub and study the back of her hair to make sure the curls meet perfect in the center, when we are getting somewhere in the medical mystery of what's wrong with me, when Dad remembers to find her in the kitchen for a kiss after work, when everything is *just right*—then he belches like a tornado and plunks down in his chair, unzips his trousers, and nestles a palm down there.

OUR STRANGE TIMES ARE PUNCTUATED with brilliant ones, too, enough of them to convince me of the happy childhood Mom and Dad say I have since kids in Africa are dropping off like flies. Times when all convention is thrown out the window and we say to hell with having turkey on Thanksgiving and cook up a bunch of shrimp instead, laughing at our quirky freedom. We are free—of relatives, neighbors, friends. Nobody can tell us what to do. We'll stick a can of Crisco in the fondue pot and tempura up a pile of cheese cubes and mushrooms for Christmas dinner. Who says we have to follow any rules?

Dad is a one-off inspirational chef. Most of his weekends are spent watching TV or tinkering in his garage, but now and then he wakes up early, has his Agent Orange puke, gets out the heavy pressure cooker pot and candy thermometer, and we make rock candy.

We have to plot how we're going to get the flavors because Mom thinks it's a waste of money, so when we're all in town, Dad and I sneak back to the pharmacy counter while Mom gets groceries and we act like espionage spies, asking in a whisper if we can see the flavors "in the back." The pharmacist plays along, looks around to see who's watching, and then covertly opens up a cabinet, where hundreds of small vials of potent flavors sit: butterscotch, tutti-frutti, strawberry, watermelon, horehound.

While Dad drains a whole bottle of Karo syrup into

the pan, I pick out the flavors from our growing collection. The pot of hard candy is poured out onto wax sheets in a big production where Dad—in big fluffy mitts up to his elbows, at the exact set second and temperature—shrieks, "Look out, Sissy! Look out!" and zooms across the kitchen to ooze the concoction onto the paper before it starts to set. I fly out of Dad's way and sprinkle the cooling candy with powdered sugar. Then Dad and I take the big sheets and strike them against the edge of the counter to make smaller ones and then I get to break them into mouth-size pieces with our drywalling hammer.

And the rest of our happy times were captured in Kodak moments as tangible proof for the world to see that we were, in every sense of the word, normal. Tucked in Christmas cards and signed with our individual names, forged in Mom's own cursive handwriting, these photos—us standing on the edge of the Painted Desert, crowded into a plywood cutout shark's mouth at Sea World, grimacing next to our horses, holding runners-up ribbons—were the casting lines out to distant relatives and long-lost friends Mom so desperately wanted to look good to.

BUT THE REAL TRUTH can be scrutinized by peering just a little closer at the small stack of pictures left over from the fire. In one Polaroid, me, Mom, and Danny sit amidst a frenzy of torn wrapping paper, under the Christmas tree—loaded with ornaments, laden with icicles—the three of us surrounded by a moat of presents: Stretch Armstrong, ballerina jewelry box, Hot Wheels loop-de-loop racetrack, Rubik's Cube, Spirograph, Mouse Trap, latch hook rug kit, boxed set of *Black Beauty and Other Classics*—all the proof of our happy Christmas. Danny wears his funny clown face, Mom cranes her neck, strains a smile. And hiding behind my own puffy eyes is the tiniest glint of what really happened that morning: Mom screeching through the trailer, threatening to commit suicide.

DANNY IS ALMOST OUT of kindergarten when Mom notices the wheeze in his chest. We always knew he was going to need tubes put in his ears and his tonsils out, like I did, but now Mom says he's got to get an inhaler since he's having such a hard time catching his breath.

"Are you okay, Danny, you sure you can breathe, honey?" Mom stands behind my little brother with her hand resting lightly on his back while he sputters and huffs.

"He can't seem to catch his breath around the house when we're home." Mom scissors a fold of Danny's thick golden hair between her fingers, and gently pulls it to the side of his face so the doctor can see him. Danny sits in the examining room with his shoulders curved into himself, occasionally gasping like a guppy out of the bowl. I sit in the other chair because Mom has to keep me home from school too. Otherwise, by the time she's done shopping, she wouldn't get back in time to see me off the bus.

"Strangely, at school, he seems to breathe fine. It must be pollen rolling in from the fields that have these asthma attacks coming on. We're surrounded down there by ragweed and clover, Doctor."

Mom has researched Danny's wheeze in the medical

books she's been collecting. She sends away for the *Time-Life* series. No commitment necessary, cancel at any time. The books stack up like a miniature winding staircase by the couch: *The Encyclopedia of Disease, Internal Organs and Their Functions, The Pill Book*. She reads late into the night, long after we've all gone to sleep, keeping an eye out for our symptoms so she can suggest the right tests and meds to the doctor.

Danny walks through the house with his white plastic inhaler stuck in his mouth.

Mom tags behind. "Are you okay, Danny? Can you breathe? Are you starting to wheeze up, sweetie? Let me put a hand on your chest and feel what's going on in there." And she holds him sandwiched between her hands, one on his back, the other rising and falling with each of Danny's wheezy gasps.

The next week, Danny lies on the couch, sucking on his inhaler like a pacifier. Dad glances over on a commercial. "Son, what the hell you got in your mouth there?"

Mom pops like a jack-in-the-box from around the kitchen partition. "Dan, this is something I've been meaning to talk to you about." She walks in to stand in front of the set. "When the TV's off.

"Dan." She pauses, licks her lips. "Your son has asthma, and you need to know what his state of health is. I can tell you right now it doesn't look good." Dad blinks and nods in agreement, then tries to remove her from in front of the set with a few airy swipes of his hand. "We'll talk about this on a break."

Mom rolls her eyes and stomps back to the kitchen. On the next commercial, Dad snaps his chair up in a great swoosh and springs out of it. I'm setting the table when the trailer shakes. I make out their torsos through the space between the cabinets and the counter. Dad grabs Mom's wrist and pins it to the counter. He leans in close, and she draws away, bending back over the sink.

"Let's get one thing straight, Sandy." He growls low. "You're going to leave Daniel Joseph Gregory the Second alone from now on. That's my boy in there," he cracks her wrist against the counter like rock candy, her cry twists my stomach, "and my boy's just fine."

Mom and Dad vehemently opposed smoking. Alcohol wasn't allowed under our roof. Mom and Dad never touched a drop. And every fall Danny and I were tugged into the living room and made to watch *Angel Dust,* the yearly antidrug program where some kid on LSD thinks he can fly and jumps from the balcony into an empty swimming pool. In slow motion. Even Dad willingly gave up his reruns to make sure we saw *Angel Dust*.

And we went to church in fresh-start spurts after weekends of beatings and taking the Lord's name in vain. But despite the straight-and-narrow, fear-of-the-wrath-of-God life we lived, authority was always something to be taken into our own hands. And with the right to bear arms.

Because as soon as we moved down to the bottom of Burns Road, Mom and Dad started stockpiling guns. We didn't have to worry about black kidnappers anymore, but Mom had read about an escaped convict who caught a Greyhound into the country and butchered a family when he wandered across their isolated farm.

Our road was so remote, Mom reasoned, that if an escaped convict got down here, there'd be nothing to stop him from murdering us, chopping us into little pieces, and sticking us out in the forty-cubic-foot freezer in the garage. Who would know? How long would it take before anyone noticed us missing?

To keep us out of the ice box, guns were stashed throughout the house: one on top of the fridge (out of little Danny's way), one in the bathroom cabinet behind the hidden Fredrick's of Hollywood catalogues, one under each of Mom and Dad's bed pillows, one in the car glove box, and another tucked under the front seat. You never knew when you might need a loaded gun.

The country was so eerily quiet that when a car pulled in to the top of our graveled road from the paved one, we could instantly hear the faint grumble of its tires, alerting us that someone was on their way. How fast they drove told us if they knew the sudden curves in the road or if this was their first time down. If it didn't sound like one of the two families that lived beyond us, Mom would stick a gun in her back pocket and peer out the rear bedroom window as the car drove past, jotting down the license plate number and calling it in to the sheriff's to run a check on it. She scattered her calls among different county departments, and any one of them would run the license on the suspicious vehicle that was staking us out—driving slowly past our property or turning around in the drive.

It got so it was just easier for Mom to carry a gun in the back pocket of her jeans all the time; that way, she didn't have to run for one when she heard strange tires. Mom pulled her gun on the one lone salesman who came to our door selling magazines. And when two teenage boys hiked back our road on a day trip, she sent Stink Pup and Ebony out to tree them, and then held them there with her pistol waving until she had thoroughly interrogated them herself.

W HEN I WAS TWELVE and as stickly as a child insect, I learned to fire a .45 at the make-believe target of a human heart Dad sketched in the air with his hand in case I ever saw a strange man on our property. Dad clasped my palms over the pearl handle of the gun and steadied my wrists, aiming the barrel at the man's imaginary chest.

Then he let go and told me to squeeze. My weak wrists shimmied from the resistance of the trigger, until finally, with my shoulders curved into my body, my knees buckled for leverage, my face clenched down, and my head drifting sideways, the gun—by now lopsided too—exploded with a little puff of metallic dust that went peppery in my nose. The back kick of the bullet alone nearly toppled me over.

LATER. MOM IS STANDING in front of the TV again. This time she's blocking _M*A*S*H,_ a sacrilege in our house.

"Sandy, Jeeeesus." Dad winces like Archie Bunker. "Can't it wait till a goddamn commercial, can't you see I'm in the middle of this?"

Danny and I teeter at the edge of the living room, stretching out over the colonial velour wagon-wheel couch on our tippy toes. "Mom, pleeease, just leave him alone, please don't do this. C'mon, Mom, please come over here."

But she stands solid, her hands ganged up on her

hips like a bunch of bananas, her torso leaning forward, that little white blob gaining speed. "If you were a man, you fat-assed faggot, you good-for-nothing, lazy-ass, son-of-a—" She flicks off the set with a superior *snap!*

Dad roars out of the La-Z-Boy like an incensed rhino and charges after her, scooping up one of the concrete animals she lines the trailer with into his wide palm. Mom races down the hall screaming. We bolt out of the way and stand helpless in the kitchen, at the mouth of the dark hallway, straining after their shadows. He catches her neck and strings her up against the wall at the end of the hall; she dangles choking, like a long, thin praying mantis. He bashes the smiling calico cat again and again into the orange velvet wallpaper as she flops her head. She's yelling, "He's gonna kill me! He's killing me!"

I snatch the gun off the fridge, grip my fingers around white mother-of-pearl. Little Danny and I race down the hall into the eye of the storm. Our mother's feet sway off the floor, her head lashing in smaller and smaller arcs as he walks his grip up her neck. He is going to bash in her skull.

I am a gazelle in slow motion, leaping down the hallway through distant time and space. I lunge toward them, and Mom's screams swallow my head. Danny flings himself around Dad's legs, his forehead pressing into Dad's groin for leverage as he beats his little fists on Dad's belly. I cock the trigger and yank my father's hair back with one hand, pushing the gun into the soft hole of his temple with the other.

"Go ahead, shoot me, you fucking bitch, pull the goddammed trigger, blow my brains all over this goddamned wall. Shooooooooot meeeeee!" He blindly hammers the concrete cat into the wall like an assembly-line machine. Holes open in the wood paneling and swallow sheets of orange velvet.

"Let her *gooooo*."

"Let him kill me, Julie, just let him put me out of my misery and kill me!"

"Noooo, Moooom! Don't go, Mommmy. Don't kill Daddd, Sis!"

Mom screams. Dad screams. Danny screams. I scream.

And there we are, slammed into the corner of the broken hallway, glued together, our throats scorched from the violent force of words meant to save each other, the four of us one tight coil to spring or wind in tandem. And as we reach a crescendo, we hover timeless; resonating in the glass-shattering acoustics torn from our chests, and then, almost in perfect unison, the tension breaks. Dad's shoulders deflate, his hand eases off Mom's neck, her feet float dreamily to the floor, the gun slides out of his temple leaving the perfect round indent of a bullet's path. Danny unhinges from Dad and there we stand, dazed, unwound, eyes glossed with adrenaline.

It is the boil-over that brings us back to a simmer.

Mom slips into her room, Dad staggers back to the TV, and Danny and I turn our backs on each other and stumble into our own rooms, diagonal from one another. School's only been out for a few days. We've got another whole week of keeping the peace before Christmas break is over.

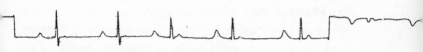

BUT THE MEMORIES THAT HANG heavi-
est are the easiest to recall. They hold
in their creases the ability to change one's life, organi-
cally, forever. Even when you shake them out, they've
left permanent wrinkles in the fabric of your soul.

It's a school night and I'm already tucked into bed. I
can tell Mom's standing in front of the television because Dad's roaring, "I'm telling you, woman, you had
better be out of my way by the time this commercial is
over. Onne. Twooo . . ."

It's hard to say what Mom wants to talk about. The
bills, us kids, my medical problems. But it's nothing that
Dad'll turn the TV off for. Or if he does, it's in a once-a-
year attempt to be a better father, a better husband, a
better man, and he clicks the set off, releases a sigh and
says, "Okay, Sandy. Seeeee, now. The set is off. What is
it that's so important you want to talk about?"

But tonight they're yelling on the commercials, and
that's a good sign. At least they're communicating. I've
got the Fingerhut and Swiss Colony catalogues under
the covers with a flashlight, one eye on the page, one ear

trained on the sounds of the trailer, picking out all the things I'm going to buy Mom as soon as I'm old enough to get a job. I'm making lists. Then diagramming my lists, with weekly payment columns and minimum payment versus interest, tallying up the things I'm gonna put in layaway, because I've thoroughly read the policy page in the middle of the catalogue and they do take payments, you know.

Every week, Mom'll get a mail-order surprise: the hundred-dollar fruit-and-petit-fours basket, or the pink terry inflatable bath pillow, or the little strawberry-wrapped candies from Swiss Colony. She'll always have something to look forward to. I cannot wait to make my mother happy.

My list is three sheets long now. I imagine Mom's face when she opens my gifts, how excited she is and how each present comes on the brink of an argument or crying spell or dead-end doctor's appointment and none of it really matters because she'll already be looking forward to the next present from me. The trailer goes silent. I'm falling down elevator floors jerking into sleep, my hand folded in between the order forms. The plastic doorknob on my bedroom door slowly squeaks open. Mom is framed in the doorway like a ghostly hologram, the hall light glowing behind her, her face in shadow. She tiptoes to the edge of my bed and turns to sit. That's when I notice the gun in her mouth, her full lips formed around the barrel of the .45 off the fridge.

She looks at me with her tear-streaked, puffy face. She holds me with her eyes, terrified like an animal in a chute, and raises her hand to cock the trigger. Her wrist shimmies just like mine did.

"Mommy, Mommy, Mommy!" I shoot from under

the covers, and start crying on cue. Mimic and match. If I mirror her with an appropriate response, she'll look in the mirror at herself, her attention distracted from the gun, even if only for a second.

She opens her lips, still with the weight of the metal barrel pressing on her tongue. "Won't you want we to will myself?"

She slides it out of her mouth. "You kids want me to kill myself, don't you?" I cry harder. "I mean you kids hate me. I'm such a bitch, such a nag as your father says and you kids hate me, that's what he says."

And now my tears have caught up for real. I'm crying for her, telling her no, we don't hate you, no, Mommy, we love you and we don't want you to kill yourself because then we couldn't have a mommy.

She drops the gun to her lap, her chin collapses to her chest. I cling around her like a baby monkey. As she deflates, I get stronger.

"Mom, if you don't live then I can't live. Okay? Okay?" trying for the nod of agreement she demands from Dad. "Who would take care of me when I'm sick, who would take me to the doctor?" I lace my voice with disgust and jab a thumb toward the La-Z-Boy. "You think *he* will?"

Mom shakes and sobs. "Have you ever been molested, Julie?"

I don't know what molested is, I'm only eyeing the gun, thinking of how I'm going to make a grab for it.

Mom hiccups and sobs. "It was Lee, him and the neighbor boy. They tied me on the workbench, got the cell batter" she wails, "reee."

My stomach is churning but I can't make out the rest of what she's saying. I hang on to her, slipping the gun so lightly from her lap she doesn't notice, sliding it under my blankets. "It's okay, it's okay, Mom."

"They hooked the clamps to my—*Oh, God,*" she sobs, "I remember screaming for Mom. She closed the basement door. She knew, Julie, she knew what was going on."

My tears are all my own now, flowing and falling; for my mother, for me, for what happened to her, for those same things she says could happen to me at the hands of men; men I know, men who might be a brother who's a little off, *wink, wink,* or my father, or a neighbor and I'm saying don't die, don't die, Mom, and making a silent promise to myself that nobody will ever touch me there—*ever*—and the harder I cry, the less my beautiful mother who I love so much and could never live a second without does. And then she stops altogether. She straightens up on my bed and blows her nose on her flannel farm shirt. He eyes are near swollen shut. She gives my knee a little squeeze and says, "Hey, thanks for listening, Sis." She rises from my bed— "Well, you better get to sleep now, honey" —and leaves me on the edge of my mattress, with a loaded gun under my covers and a face as marked by her life as her own.

She turns in the doorway, "Isn't your father a no-good son of a bitch for turning you kids against me?"

"I know, Mom, I know."

EVEN THOUGH IT'S A NEW medical center, Mom knows what to do. She sits me in the waiting room and makes her way to the desk. She whispers through the reception window that I'm shy about my symptoms. She better speak to the doctor private.

I sit on the examining room table, in a big man's gown, swinging my legs against the cold metal sides. I'm waiting. How weird I had to take off my undies. I never did that at Township. Mom is somewhere out there, with the doctor.

A nurse knocks lightly and peeks in. "Okay, Miss Gregory. Can you follow me now, hon? We're going to another room down the hall."

It's a larger exam room, dimly lit. The table sits in the center and next to it stands a different nurse with a metal tray. I sit on the table and the nurse at my side takes ahold of my shoulders and pushes me back until I'm lying down. *That's odd.* As I'm adjusting on the paper, trying not to wrinkle it for them, the nurse who came and got me rolls her stool over to the bottom of the table and wraps her icy fingers around my ankles, stretching them away from me.

"Now I'm just going to have you put your feet into these stirrups. It might be a little cold." I'm thinking, Stirrups? How can they have saddle stirrups in here? as the nurse slips my bare heels into what feels like the shoe sizer in good department stores.

"What're you doing? What're you going to do to me today?" They always tell me what they're about to do. Without a word, the nurse at my side ties my arm with a clear rubber hose. She smoothes an alcohol pad over the thin skin of the crook of my arm and taps for a vein.

The nurse at my feet says, "Now this might be a little stick, Julie. We've got to get this plastic tube into the urethra 'cause Mom says you can't go."

My heart is pounding; what's urethra? What is she

doing down there? I open my mouth to ask, but a startled scream rips out instead.

"Now, Julie, I can't do this if you don't stay still for me."

She jabs at me with a hard plastic straw.

My limbs retreat like a spider's, curling in to protect soft belly, to keep spindly legs from snapping off. The silent nurse at my side stretches my wrist out, to make the soft pad of my vein arch to the needle. She pushes the plunger. My blood sears with hot liquid, blazing through me.

"Julie. Stop it!" the nurse at my feet commands. "I know it's a shock, but be a good girl and let's get this over with. Hold still for me now."

I hook my free arm over my face, bite, suck, gnaw on it. I heave uncontrollably like a distressed infant. My head lashes side to side. The nurse at my feet mumbles something about how an injection of iodine dye will color my urine so she can see how it flows. Slobber and snot and tear slick smear the crook of my arm while the rubber sheath unsnaps my other one, offering it back, limp, used.

The nurse at the foot of the table slides out at the same time. "We've done it. Now see? That wasn't so bad, now was it?"

My eyes are clamped shut; sealed with sticky tears. I unpeel them to hot lights. I'm floating, slowly, back to my body. *Where am I?* A mound is rising up on my wet face and I touch it, then one on my arm bubbles up, another on my face. I'm itching a crop of red, pulsating hives creeping over my face, neck, arms, and thighs. The nurse leads my mother into the room. She is soft and smiling, asking her if I was good. I'm itching like crazy, tearing at the welts, swallowing my cow's tongue.

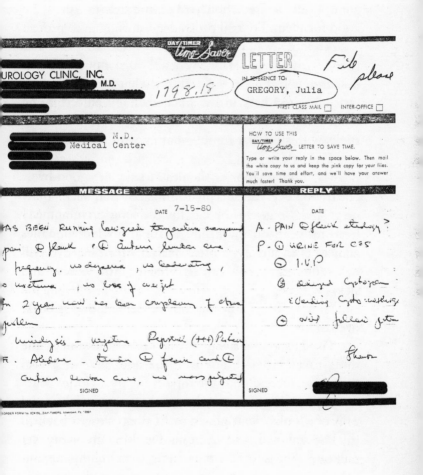

UROLOGY CLINIC, INC.
_____ M.D.

1798.15

LETTER

File please

IN REFERENCE TO:
GREGORY, Julia

FIRST CLASS MAIL ☐   INTER-OFFICE ☐

_____ M.D.
Medical Center

HOW TO USE THIS
DAY/TIMER *time-Saver* LETTER TO SAVE TIME.
Type or write your reply in the space below. Then mail
the white copy to us and keep the pink copy for your files.
You'll save time and effort, and we'll have your answer
much faster! Thank you.

MESSAGE | **REPLY**

DATE 7-15-80

...AS BEEN Running low grade ~~temperature everning~~
pain ® flank & ℗ anterior lumbar area
frequency, no dysuria, no bedwetting,
no urethra, no loss of weight
for 2 years now has been complaining of chronic
problem
  Urinalysis - negative Dipstick (+++) Protein
E. Abdomen - tender ® flank and ℗
  anterior lumbar area, no mass palpated

SIGNED

DATE

A - PAIN ® flank etiology?
P - ① URINE FOR C&S
   ② I.V.P
   ③ delayed Cystogram :
      Voiding Cysto-urethrogram
   ④ will follow patient

Thanks

SIGNED _____

ORDER FORM No. 82419L, DAY-TIMERS, Allentown, Pa. 18001

"Hmmmm," the head nurse mutters under her breath, "must have an allergy to the iodine dye." She marks my chart and slips out the door.

My mother flips through a magazine, popping her gum. "Get dressed, honey. The nurse says you were good for them. I'm real proud of you, Sis."

I cannot speak. The wires in my brain are black and fried. I cannot find language, although my hands are desperately feeling in the dark for what it is I've lost. A little drool gathers in the pocket of my parted, hung mouth. I'm disconnected from my fingers, those curling sticks with skin that fumble shakily with the buttons of stiff Wranglers.

My mother stops at the desk to say her good-byes. She thanks everyone deeply for this last-minute appointment and we get in the car for the long drive home. I lean my head on the inside of the car window. Mom glances over, furrows a brow, feels my forehead.

"You feeling all right, sweetheart? You look a little sick."

"I, have a . . . a headache." So faint it barely floats over to her.

"Well, here, let me give you one of those migraine thingys." She pats around on the floor for her purse, digs through, and pops the top off the prescription vial.

"Here, honey, we better give you a double dose. This one looks like it's the worst I've ever seen on you."

She smiles bright, her eyes twinkle glitter into my dull ones. She is thrilled to be here, at the right place and time, to anticipate and treat my illness with the right medication.

"I'm so glad I'm here to witness this, Julie. Now I can tell them what happens at the onset of one of these nasty doo-dahs."

I look out the window and the air between us fades as the fields gain sideways momentum and begin to blur by. I'm on a Tilt-A-Whirl in my still life. My mother drives serene and calm, her smiling head bent slightly to the side, thinking about a private funny between her and the nurse. The sun shines in on my side and without the cold spring air, it warms my head like an angel breathing hot on my scalp. I pass out in the light of her breath and drool down the window.

I THINK JULIE NEEDS KIDS to play with, Dan." Dad's on the couch, the TV's off. It's one of his "I'm going to be a better father-husband-person" forty-eight-hour stints and Mom is telling him that with all my missed school and the uncertainty of my sickness, if I don't get some kids my own age to play with, I'm not going to develop any social skills that will let me interact normally with others out in the real world.

IT'S TEN O'CLOCK IN THE MORNING and the caseworker will be here any second. Mom runs around the house. "How do I look? Julie, goddamn it, pick up this bathroom!"

Dad stands by the hutch in the foyer dressed in his light blue outfit and new white loafers. He waits for her command, anything that gives him direction and makes him useful. He crosses his wrists, as if tying them up would keep him from smudging the freshly lemon-waxed furniture.

A car pulls in at the top of the road. Everybody freezes, like a den of rabbits, ears perked, trying to recognize the tones under the tires. Two more seconds and we'll know if it's her.

"Okay." Mom snaps into action. "Everybody act normal. Kids, you stay inside. If the caseworker talks to you, tell them that what you want most are little brothers and sisters to play with, to share the horses with. Dan, let's get out there. Get a move on."

She pushes past Dad and runs out the front door of the trailer, "Dan! Come onnn." She stamps her foot at him, like an impatient horse pawing.

Once in sight of the driveway, she walks slow and casual. Mom clasps the caseworker's hand; Dad stands in the shadow, a few steps behind. They show her around: the pool, the ponies, the pond—just stocked with trout so the kids can go fishing—yeah, a real kid haven, Mom laughs softly.

"We love kids, and can't have any more—we were foster parents in Arizona years ago and, you know— thought we might get back into it now that we're settled here."

Mom does all the talking. The caseworker is tall, skinny, and soft. She looks like a walking, talking Holly Hobbie doll, wearing her big glasses that magnify her eyeballs and dressed in her to-the-ankle flowery skirt, and little slip-on shoes with soft soles. Too soft even for her to walk across the cheap, razor-sharp gravel in our driveway. She giggles at this as she walks around the drive and along the grass. She is taken by this shining family, this diamond in the coal mines of southern Ohio, where finding a foster family with all their teeth intact is a plus, let alone all the amenities that come with the Gregory family.

"Yes, I think this would be lovely," she says, looking

around. "You've got quite a serene place out here, so remote and quiet. Now, you can take how many of our children? You're building on how many more bedrooms?"

Mom talks, cocks her head, leans in to the caseworker, articulates with her hands, lightly touches the woman's arm. Dad follows, trying to look, to feel like a dad; capable of getting respect from his children, admiration from his wife, fixing things, getting things done in life.

The caseworker is captured in the kindness, cannot see past the fake wood paneling, cannot see past the locked door where Mr. Beck sits stiff in the recliner in his insulin-induced glaze, with his white loafers identical to my father's and his outfit of peed-in dried underwear he's had on all week. She can't see on top of the refrigerator, or in the bathroom cabinet or under the bed pillow, where the loaded guns are kept. And she can't see that the beautiful blond hair on my mother is really a wig ordered from the back of the Fredrick's of Hollywood catalogue because all girls with dark hair are sluts and baby makers.

Holly Hobbie is soft in her demeanor, too soft to notice the sharp edges that get lost in the country-time slowness of our farm. Twenty minutes is all it takes, and she is caught.

Hook, line, and sinker.

NOW THAT WE'RE GETTING foster kids, we're all going to have to do better. We load up in the wagon one Sunday morning and head for the Laurelville Church of God. We stand in the pews and sing as a family. Dad doesn't pass the plate down our row empty, and he doesn't pretend to sell Buicks during the sermon, either, trying to crack me and Danny up. On the ride home, he and Mom talk in the front seat about how we're going to start going to church every Sunday from here on out, starting right now today.

That night, in the bathtub, I think about what the preacher said, how God is watching over every one of us in everything we do. I wonder about God watching me now, down on Burns Road, sitting in the yellow plastic bathtub filled with rusty well water. I wonder if he thinks I'm spending too much time in here. I wonder if he thinks I'm using enough soap. And as I wonder about all the other things God sees me do that I'm not sure if I want him to, the crown of my head starts to heat up. The feeling is warm and slow and my eyes gently drift closed, almost like feathery fingertips have grazed down over my lids. I sit slack in the water while warmth bathes me from above, rolling over my shoulders, easing down my arms, hitting the surface and radiating in a circle around me. I squint my eyes shut and lift my face to the ceiling. I know he's up there, watching. And that warm delirious feeling is straight from God's bucket. God is up there, watching over me, pouring a bucket of pure golden light right down on top of my head. It's too bright to even open my eyes. I'm smiling to God because right then I know that everything, somehow, is going to be all right.

MOM AND I ARE AT THE NEW PEDIATRI-cian in town, the first and only female I ever see.

"Julie's been having a lot of indigestion lately—I'd say the loudest belching I've ever heard outta any kid. Haven't you, Julie? And she seems to have an adverse reaction to meat, almost like her system can't tolerate it. Her father has tried to get her to eat meat and she actually throws right up. Don't you, Sis? Nobody around here can figure out what's wrong with the kid. God, I hope you can help us. These small-town doctors don't take this serious, you know? I don't think they're as competent and diligent as you'll be."

This is our second visit to Dr. Kate in one week. The first one was for a tetanus booster when I stepped barefoot on a rusty nail. Mom's got me in today for my indigestion.

"Okay, Julie, let's just have you stand up for me now and see what your heart's doing."

"Hmmm, do that again."

I'M WINDED. I'M HUNGRY. It's two o'clock and I haven't eaten yet today. I was going to school without breakfast, not getting any lunch money, and when I got off the bus at home, I had to do all the farm work: feed the horses, haul three bales of hay from the barn to the manger, chop the ice in the trough with a mallet, feed the horses buckets of grain, and put an extra one in the car for that colt we fed on the way to town, then feed and water all the little dogs that lived with matted and muddy coats out in the pens. Once the animals were done, I had to load up the rug inside with enough firewood to last the night and the next day and dump out the tray of ash from the bottom of the wood-burning stove. Sometimes Dad would get up and hold the door open while I teetered, bearing the weight of the full ash pan against my chest. Then I had to chop wood with an ax to re-place what I'd put in the house and then lug in five-gallon buckets of coal I had to shovel off the pile. When I came in, I had to set the table for dinner and clean up afterward. Mom said Danny was too little to be out there around the horses and besides, all that hay and coal dust was bad for his asthma and she'd just got him well enough that she didn't have to run him to the doc-tors anymore. The foster kids were usually hiding in their bedroom, doing homework. I could only do my homework after I did everything else and that usually wasn't until late. And sometimes the next morning Mom kept me home anyway because she was trying to get me in to see a doctor that day.

And just today I got busted for stealing mixed fruit from a kid's tray in the school cafeteria. As a sixth-grader, you could work in the lunch room for a free meal if you signed up in homeroom early enough. Most days my bus got me to school way too late to get on the list, but today I'd got lucky. I was washing dishes; spraying off the leftovers and stacking the trays on the conveyer belt. I knew the kid; he was the little brother of a girl in my class. He handed me his tray and asked if I wanted his fruit cup. It was against cafeteria rules to take food off the trays when they got handed over but it looked so good, and who was going to see me? I bent down and just scooped it off into my cupped fingers and let the syrup of canned fruit flow down my throat. I swallowed the peaches whole and sucked on the pear cubes until they became grainy in my mouth. It was delicious.

But the kid in the cafeteria told on me. He said I could have his fruit and when I gorged on it, he trotted straight over to tell old Ms. Sweeney that I stole his food. I was two years older. I knew the cafeteria rules. And Ms. Sweeney made me read an apology to him out loud in front of the whole class. I trudged to his classroom after lunch, a lunch I didn't get because I wasn't allowed to work in the cafeteria anymore. I read the letter while my stomach growled so loud half the class laughed. And when I started crying half way through, Ms. Sweeney let me off the hook.

How could I tell Dr. Kate that I didn't have lunch money? That since the foster kids got state lunches, Mom said I should, too. Why waste a dollar twenty when the school should be paying for me to eat? But Mom said I must have lost the first set of vouchers I brought home for her to sign, and the second set sat tucked in the kitchen cabinet, waiting for her to fill them out. I stole bits of change out of her purse, but Little Debbie snack cakes were all I could get. I sneaked tablespoonfuls of Cool Whip from the fridge for breakfast and ate the junk my coins got me at lunch.

I was the one popping the change from the Franklin Mint coin collector books Dad had started for Danny and kept tucked away in the bottom of the hutch: punching out dimes and clawing out a quarter at a time. God help me if he found out.

"THERE'S A SUBSTANTIAL DIFFERENCE in Julie's heart rate when she stands up from when she's at rest, Ms. Gregory."

Mom nods furiously.

"And just in watching her, she seems to have difficulty breathing when she stands. How does it feel upon rising, Julie?"

"Tell her how out of breath you are, Julie. She's always out of breath around the farm, Dr. Kate. *Jesus,*" Mom slaps her knee, "this explains everything."

"My heart beats fast and I feel maybe a little dizzy."

"You look like you're about ready to pass out, hon," Mom says. "Don't you feel like you could pass out?"

"Well, Ms. Gregory, I think we might have something for the hospital here, something that could be detected with a simple EKG, EEG, or a heart exam. They might even want to attach something called a Holter monitor on her overnight to see the longer rhythms of her heart. I'll call over to the cardiac unit and get you set up. Is that all right with you, Sandy?"

"YESS-YEEESSSS." MOM'S THUMPING the steering wheel. "Finally, we're getting somewhere. I knew that Dr. Kate was a good one. These stupid good old boys wouldn't know their ass from a hole in the ground. I knew there was something major going on with you."

We're going to the hospital! It is all pretty exciting, we're *this* close. In the cardiac ward they lay me out on a table and hook little soft white pads to my chest. These are wired into a machine, and I just lie there, quietly breathing, while the machine does what it's supposed to do. I'm hooked up, staring at the ceiling. *At last, I'll just take one medication that will fix everything. I'll have friends, be in sports, go to movies. Mom'll be happy; she won't have to stay at home or clean up after old men or foster kids. And I'll be a real kid and not miss school anymore.*

That was what I wanted the most; to do good in school like I used to after Danny was born, before I got sick again.

Since we moved to Burns Road, I've been demoted to the lowest reading level. I got paddled by my teacher

y 9, 1982

M. D.
Drive
umbus, Ohio

Julie Gregory
D.: 05-16-69
: 13 yrs., 2 mo.
ents: Dan & Sandra Gregory
13621 Burns Rd.
Amanda, Ohio

erred for symptomatic arrhythmia::

eral sxs of tired all the time, no stamina, can't keep up with other kids.

sodic sxs of about 3 years duration occurring approximately 3 times/month
ting 15-20 minutes characterized by sharp chest pain, SOB, anxiety and a feeling
t her heart "races and skips". Her mother verifies that her heart is racing
lse of 128-144-167 during episodes) and describes her as ashen in the face.
ently her episodes (or awareness of them) have increased in frequency to once
twice a day.

t history includes "indigestion" since she was an infant. GI workup has been
e in the past and reported as negative. Hematuria occurred on one occassion,
ribed to a viral cystitis. Arm fractures twice from falls.

: Can't eat meat- causes vomiting
Frequent nausea- seems to be relieved by candy
Frequently feels dizzy when assuming upright position

ergies: Iodine dye- hives

ily History: Julie's mother has palpitations which she can stop by applying
essure on her eyeballs

Julie's MGM has also had palpitations. Her PGF and PGM had diabetes. Her
died at 42 years.

Julie's tall thin habitus is not a family trait.

sical: Pulse rates were 82, 76, 88 at various times in the office. Immediately
n standing she ran 128. After running she was 140 and regular with recovery
resting rate in 2 minutes.
B. P. 100/68. Resp. 24.
Ht. 63 1/4 (50-75%), arm span 65 1/2 (90-95%), wt. 86 (10-25%)
Marfanoid habitus.
General physical exam is WNL.

Work up: Standard 12 lead EKG, 5 hour glucose tolerance test, and chest x-ray
normal. Holter Monitor, 24 hours confirms variations in rhythm with both
bradycardia and tachycardia.

Question:
1. Do you agree her symptomotology is related to her arrhythmia?
2. Does she have mitral valve prolapse, sick sinus syndrome, or
   another arrhythmia mechanism?
3. Would Inderal or another antiarrhythmic improve her ability to partic

Please discuss your findings with Julie and her mother. Please handle her med
tions, if any, from there.

I will be glad to arrange Holter monitoring again for on going evaluation.

I would appreciate a copy of your consultation and a report on her M-mode or
2 D ECHO if you feel this is indicated.

Thank you.

Sincerely,

Addendum - Nov. 23, 1982

Dr. ▮▮▮ (see letter) has since recommended furt
studies. Essentially no change on medications.
What were sometimes ascribed to changes (slow
etc.) due to the medication are probably just a
explained by the family now focusing more attent
to her pulse rates during various periods of sympto

The same three questions remain as above.
Can we improve her quality of life or give her
more guidance in accepting and adjusting her
expectancies to her capacity?

Thank you.

for getting a D on a science test. Mom says this school is harder, but it's not. The teacher is fat and stupid and I get problems wrong because I'm looking for the clever answers in what I think are trick questions. I blurt out the advanced answer, but it's always the simple one.

And I'm failing at school because I'm sick; because there's always something wrong with me.

ELL, MS. GREGORY, we've got good news. The Holter monitor shows no significant findings that lead us to believe Julie has a heart condition requiring further tests. Nothing outside a normal parameter." The hospital doctor is following the zigzags on my chart, showing us what he can't find. Mom slaps her leg.

"What? What do you mean, you can't find anything?" She counts on her fingers the number of things leading up to this moment. "Dr. Kate called you, she told you this kid had a racing heart, was out of breath all the time. She told me we were going to get helped here, that we'd finally be able to get to the bottom of things. What are you trying to tell me here, that this kid is normal? That I'm making this up?"

"No, we didn't say any—"

"Well, let me tell you, let me tell you. I'm going to find a doctor competent enough to find out what's wrong with her, you understand me? I'm going back to Dr. Kate and tell her that you people just don't give a rat's ass about this kid."

MOM DOESN'T TRUST THE SMALL-TOWN HOSPITAL; not with their country manner, their outdated equipment, and their normal test results. We drive to Dr. Kate's, an emergency walk-in. I stand up. I sit down. Dr. Kate hears the same race, the same shortness of breath, the same exertion from effort.

Mom rails while Kate presses her stethoscope to my heart. "I mean she just can't keep up. You know? I mean you'd think I was working her to death or starving her or something. I fix good meals, she doesn't eat. I mean what am I supposed to do, force her to eat, shove food down her throat?"

"Ms. Gregory, I'm sure you're doing the best you can. Some kids are just finicky. And if it's a heart condition, it'll explain a lot of your anxiety. Stand up for me again, Julie."

"I mean I try to get her into 4-H, she's tired. We get in the car, she's carsick, has a headache. I mean, I'm a good mother, what did I do to deserve this? Why am I being punished?"

"Sandy," Dr. Kate rolls her little button chair over to Mom, "I have every intention of finding you another cardiologist to take Julie to. I've got one in mind associated with one of the best cardiac units in the country, Ohio State University. I'm sure you're doing a great job with Julie." She turns to me in kiddie talk: "Isn't she, Julie. Tell Mom she's doing a great job. Say, 'Hey, Mom, don't worry, we'll get it all straightened out!'" She turns back to Mom. "When you have a sick child, it can really test your wits. I'll do my best to get through to the right person that can help find out what's wrong with Julie."

Mom unburies her head from her hands, dabs an eye. "Thank you, Dr. Kate. I just have so much guilt, that it's something I'm not doing right, that I should do more, but I just can't, I can't be good enough. I'm bending over backwards here and we just aren't getting anywhere. Nobody's listening. Nobody's doing anything to help me, you know?"

"Sandy, you're a great mother and I think you're doing a terrific job with Julie. We're all in this together. I'll help you get to the bottom of this. I promise."

I ALWAYS WANTED TO BE ONE of those clean, pretty girls, whose clothes stayed jelly-free and unwrinkled, with long shaped nails, no dirty rind underneath from shoveling coal or hauling in wood.

But instead I was long and lanky and everything about me was greasy and stringy, tangled and tired. I tried out for cheerleading but couldn't even do a measly banana split. Once I got down, I couldn't quite get back up.

I took bicycling in seventh-grade gym but usually spent the class sitting on the bench, winded and tuckered out, my stick legs swimming in the smallest-size red polyester gym shorts McDowell Middle School offered.

No matter how hard I tried I ended up in situations that only accentuated my awkwardness. I was on my hands and knees one day in school, markering on a banner that lay outstretched on the cafeteria floor. I was hunched over, coloring; open mouth, lazy tongue drooping into the bowl of a bottom lip slung wide. Heavy glazed eyes; each breath from my lungs pumped as laboriously as if it had been the handle of our well being primed.

When I slid my hand across the paper, the color smeared.

I couldn't figure out where the water was coming from. Then I noticed a puddle on the paper and a fishing line flowing upwards. I traced the line with my eyes all the way to my bottom lip. I had drooled without noticing.

And the older I got, the worse I got. My possible conditions expanded to include genetic disorders and heart valve malfunctions. And the medications to treat them piled up in the kitchen cabinets. Little pills got slipped under my tongue or dropped into my palm whenever Mom said it was time for my meds.

"Did we give you your beta blocker this morning, Sis?"

I can't remember.

"If we didn't, we better make sure we get one of those in ya."

It's just a little pill. Sometimes I don't take any, sometimes I get a double dose. I can't tell if it helps. I just feel sick all the time. The bones in my face hurt, my eyelids droop. I never stop feeling sick and I never get better. It just washes over me in various degrees of intensity. Queasy, nauseated, clammy, stupid.

BY THE TIME I WAS IN JUNIOR HIGH, Mom had built on our old doctor's suggestion of food allergies and decided I was allergic to a lot of things. She used to make me dip-your-toast-in-eggs with crispy edges every morning, and I'd sop up every bit of yolk with a soft piece of buttery toast. But now she doesn't cook me breakfast anymore. I root around in the fridge and dig out the carton of eggs.

"Julie, what the heck are you doing with those? You know you're allergic!"

I slide the eggs back and reach for the bacon.

"At-at-at, we just got done telling Dr. Kate how meat makes you sick. Why don't you just have a bowl of Sugar Pops? But use the powdered milk, just mix up enough to get them wet, you could be lactose intolerant."

Mom ordered rolls and rolls of silver-foiled weight-gain wafers from the backs of women's magazines, trying to put some pounds on me. I'd munch on them throughout the day, but they really didn't add much weight and my body shot up like a weed anyway.

Some days after school, Mom would mix up a big bowl of cookie dough from scratch or use the beaters to fix a box of cake batter.

"Here, Sis, come taste this. Isn't that good? You can take the bowl in there and watch TV with Danny if you want. Take a break from outside and get warmed up."

I shoved great heaping tablespoons of devil's food cake batter straight from the bowl into my mouth, growing sleepier and sleepier. I licked the last of the cookie dough off my fingers and scraped the final silky ribbons of yellow cake mix from the sides of the bowl. By the time I was done, I was stuffed.

But I felt even more out of it.

I was having a hard time breathing through my nose, so my mouth hung open and that made me look all the more lazy. I could hardly drag myself out in the winter to do all the work.

Mom even thought I was on drugs. I had to swear on the Bible that I was not smoking funny weed and it was just my sickness getting worse that was making me act so crazy.

I couldn't pay attention when she talked. She'd ask me to repeat back what she'd said but I couldn't remember.

And every time there was a test at school, one that I'd missed knowing about because I'd been at the doctor's, I suddenly felt faint with a headache. As the teacher walked down the aisles, passing out tests, I gimped from my chair to the nurse's office and eased onto the sickroom cot, curling under the school-issue blanket like a pill bug, trying to keep warm and just sleep.

MOM HAD BEEN BLEACHING ME BLOND for years because she knew how people saw dark-haired girls: little baby-makers just asking for it. White blond meant innocent; before the basement. She usually had me done at Hair Happening, where women no less than eighty gave me a fluorescent tint, and then she did touch-ups at home herself. She'd don the milky plastic gloves and pour lightener onto my roots, rubbing it in with her fingertips to get rid of every last smidgen of brown.

"Sandy, Jesus Christ, will you just leave the girl's hair alone? Stop turning her into a freak."

"She looks like a slut, Dan, with those dark roots, and don't you take the Lord's name in vain with me. The girl needs to be blond!"

"But she's not blond now, is she? She's green!"

This was all over a dye job that went down bad.

"Oh, right! Like those stupid junior high kids are going to notice a dark green tint. Give me a fucking break! They're kids, Daaaann. You are nuts, Dan, just nuts!"

This time at Hair Happening, I'd lucked out with

Lancaster's only gay hairdresser. He held my fried ends up and said, "This is a no-no."

Between our doubly dosed chlorine-drenched pool, the hard well water of the farm, and the constant bleaching, my hair looked like a decorative hearth broom. But Mom was the paying customer. When he swiveled me around to the mirror, my head had turned a toxic nauseating hue of burnt orange. The hairdresser pleaded with her, "For God's sake, don't do anything else to it for six months. It's going to fall out."

My hair literally glowed. Mom drove straight to the grocery store and we walked the long aisle of hair color, with her doing primary mixing in her head, trying to figure out how to get me blond again.

Chestnut Roasting was her choice. She reasoned if she put the brown over the orange, she'd get yellow. But the whole of my head turned a deep, bile green with an electrifying hint of copper. Sea plankton would have nested in there if I'd gone swimming. After those fatal results—fatal for any chance I might have had at being popular in my entire junior high school life—she gave me a choice: Go back to school as is or wear one of her blond wigs. Mom insisted that seventh- and eighth-graders just weren't savvy enough to notice hair color that defied nature or even entire synthetic scalps of hair, molded into semipermanent shapes with names like "Barb" and "Platinum."

WHEN I GET ON THE BUS the next morning, it's pitch black. But as dawn rises light into the windows, kids are going, "Heeeyyy, is your hair green?"

"Uhh, no!"

But I can't hide. Each kid that gets on is checking out

a head of hair never seen before at McDowell Middle School. I rush off the bus into school, as if speed alone will keep me invisible, but instead I am a blur of putrid green sprite darting through the halls. Kids laugh and point. I'll be banished, ridiculed, eaten alive. How am I going to survive this?

In homeroom, Missy Morrison, my one link to the insiders' track with the popular kids, laughs hysterically and tells the class I'm totally punked out, just like these super-cool videos she's seen on MTV. She's one of the few kids who gets cable—and some don't even have a TV—so her opinion turns the tide.

I'm trying to tone the whole thing down. And Missy thinks it's so cool that I'm not bragging, but actually laying low on the praise, like only a cool, green-haired, unfettered true *nuevo* visionary would do.

Before the day is out, I'm some sort of hero, having sent a message to the student body about freedom to do what you want despite the norm, choice to express whatever you feel, and control over how you want to look. There's no way I'm telling them my mom did it, and they wouldn't believe me anyway. For the first time since fourth grade I've got friends. I revel in the attention, ink notes to Missy in big fat cursive letters. Our handwriting morphs to match one another's. I slip into my new identity the moment my foot leaves the last step of my hillbilly bus. I sign my six-page letters to Missy Morrison: *Friends Forever.*

THE FOSTER KIDS WERE A CONSTANT source of uneasiness, radiating an insecurity that Danny and I often took advantage of. They would stand in pictures with feet perfectly together, spines rod-straight, hands aligned symmetrically in front of them, as if faultless body posture alone could win them the approval and acceptance of being part of a family. They shined faultless unnatural smiles, pulling back their lips to thrust out perfectly lined-up teeth at the camera. They always wanted so desperately to fit into the picture, but they never did. No matter how young they were or how long they'd been with us, they never crossed the bloodline. And they didn't get called by their individual names unless they were in trouble. Instead they were just "the foster kids," as in "We're coming up with the foster kids" or "I've got to take the foster kids with me today." Danny and I felt the split between "us" and "them" early on, but even though we hated them at first, we still tried to at least call them by their first names.

Over the next six years, we had a small crew of them: Timmy, Penny, Bradley, Rudy, Janey, Martin, Ricky, Lloyd, and later Maria. Lloyd stuttered, some of them had learning disabilities, and all of them had been removed from their own homes for some kind of abuse or neglect. They came and went. Some stayed for years while others breezed in and back out again on the revolving door of being an unruly child. Mom had a good track record with the agency because she'd take any kid the caseworker called us with, and she'd take them that day, that hour even, but she quickly weeded out the older ones by sending them back. What determined if they stayed was how young they were and how docile they could be made.

Maria was the last one to join us, and she was my favorite. With her tiny features and her little voice, she was always trying to help, to make things better, to do whatever was needed to keep everybody happy, even when it meant splitting herself into tiny pieces and trying on multitudes of characters, depending on who she was with, what position they'd taken in relationship to Mom, and how Mom was reacting to it. And it was her pictures that shone the brightest. For everything that happened to her under that roof, she built a parallel outreach into the world with her smile and kindness and the loyalty of a pound puppy. She was determined not to lose hope.

And sooner or later, each of those foster kids seemed to develop a medical mystery of their own; some traveling the well-worn path to my one-shot old doctors, with the same symptoms, getting the same tests, until we were all on a slow-roasting rotisserie that even Mom could barely keep up with. Luckily, their medical expenses were picked up by the child welfare system.

ONE DAY MOM KEPT ME HOME to go with her to one of Lloyd's appointments. I heard him scream and whimper clear down the hall into the waiting room. Nobody had to tell me what was happening. He was getting a tube shoved into his urethra and injected with that burning iodine dye; the color, the feel, of liquid scorch. A flavor you can taste in your blood, without your tongue. He was nine. I heard him scream and an electric sickness shot down the wire into my own belly. I shot up board stiff in my chair and snapped my knees together.

When Lloyd came out, he walked funny, bowlegged and to the side. He could only look at the carpet. I studied the checkout desk where Mom was waiting for him. She put her hand on his shoulder, asked if he was all right.

Nobody talked in the car. Mom made a few jokes but Lloyd and I couldn't muster the fake it would take to even pretend we weren't both sickened, he by the fact that somebody'd put a tube in his privates, me by the fact that I'd had the same thing done. We both felt the shame, but we occupied secret bubbles, separate from one another.

"Well, goddammit! Why do I even try for you ungrateful bastards? I was going to take you out to Long John Silver's but to hell with it. I try my damnedest to make sure you kids are healthy and this is how you treat me. Like shit."

"No, Mom," I pipe up, "I'm just carsick, that's all. We'd like to go to Long John's."

"Well, Lloyd, you got anything back there to say for yourself?" She glares into the backseat down at Lloyd, so tiny and faint.

"Ye-yes, San-ney, I'll-I'll-I'll go-go out to eat."

"Hmp, I bet you will, you stuttering little creep."

HOW LONG CAN YOU STARVE without side effects? If everyone around you tells you you're sick, if they keep testing you for what's making you sick, do you think, when you're thirteen, that you aren't? You feel sick, right? It's true what Mom says. You can't keep up. You are tired. Isn't there something wrong with you if you feel sick all the time? If you miss school by going to doctors and miss school by lying in the nurse's office half the day? Is it the wrong medication that makes you sick? Or the three different kinds you take all at once?

My childhood wish has come true; I have turned paper thin and translucent, as if a strong wind could whisk me high into a blue fall sky like a brittle veined maple leaf.

Mom goes to parent-teacher conferences and meets with my teachers individually about my heart condition. I hear the story, over and over. My stabs of chest pain, my shortness of breath; causing low oxygen to my brain, which explains why I'm doing poorly in school. I sit in the chair next to her, sucking air in through my hanging mouth. I just want to lie down and fade away. They are to keep an eye on me and send me home if I look faint. Teachers slice me a sideways glance as my sunken collarbone and accordion frame slink through the halls.

"*Watch her,*" they're thinking, "*she could go anytime.*"

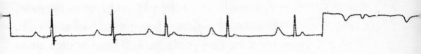

IN A WORLD OF BLOOD DRAWN and tubes shoved and veins seared with needles, of meds and headaches and missing school, of flunking and sneaking off to the nurses' office when another test comes up, how long before you start to help them find the cause? How long before you start to look through medical journals like Mom does and read about your symptoms so you can give the doctor some ideas of what to check for? How long before you get off your ass, be an adult, and start helping the people who are trying to help you?

WE'RE ON OUR WAY TO THE NEW CARDIOLOGIST, Mom white-knuckled at the wheel. This will be the third and final one Dr. Kate has sent us to, and we've waited months to see him. If he can't find anything, Dr. Kate says, it's probably not my heart.

"I'll show those goddamn no-good sons a bitches at the hospital that I'm not crazy. You are sick, goddammit, you've got a heart problem, I knew it all along, and those assholes over there at that country-bumpkin hospital don't know what the hell they're talking about."

"I know, Mom, I know. Don't worry, we'll get to the bottom of it."

"Well, we are going to go see this guy and get to the bottom of this, for Christ's sake." We slam into a parking space, she unfolds from the car and ruffles the heat out of her top; smoothes down her white slacks.

"C'mon now, let's get in there, and I mean now, goddammit." She pins me to the trunk of the car with a glare. "You are going to tell him what's wrong with you, what's happening to your heart. You understand me? Sharp chest pain. Shortness of breath. You got it?"

"Yes, Mom. I'll tell him."

WE SIT IN THE ROOM waiting for the doctor. He breezes in, spends five minutes, breezes out. He's young. Good-looking. He doesn't spend much time but gives Mom his undivided attention and concerned, perplexed facial expressions. My mother gives him her own concerned, perplexed facial expressions. Their concerned, perplexed facial expressions ricochet off of each other. She immediately calms. He's going to do another heart monitor. We're going to keep it on me double the length of time, just as Mom suggests. He signs off, slapping the chart into the plastic container on the door. My mother sighs; finally we are going to get to the bottom of this thing. I'm happy, too. As I was sitting on the examining table waiting for him, I started to think, maybe it's not my heart. Maybe it's something like my appendix. There was a kid in school who had to get his taken out and he was fine after that. Just as I was about to squeak up, the doctor strode in.

Now that he's going to do another test, I know he's on the right path. *He's so confident. He'll take care of everything. I can't believe I thought we were wrong. I don't want to have new doctors. So I have to wear the monitor for two days instead of one, so what? At least somebody will now find out what's wrong with me, instead of those stupid doctors who don't know anything.*

They lather me up. Mom steps out. The Bic slides down my chest. I hover above, think of Dad and his lathering brush, Agent Orange pukes, watch the girl who is getting her chest shaved, only she can't see me because I watch her from around the corner of the room, peering in from the hall. They squeeze the jelly on, press round white wafers on top, tape them down. The wires jut out my pants zipper. I'm so glad I don't have to go to school like this.

On the way out, my mother is humbly thankful. She emits a subtle radioactive electro-undercurrent of thrill that we're making progress. And she has decided to send me to school after all; my teachers need to see just how serious this heart condition is.

In the car we ride home in silence. I gulp air down, belch it back up. Mom reaches over and gently tucks a strand of loose hair behind my ear. Her soft graze sends electrifying goose bumps spilling down the side of my body. *We are going to get to the bottom of this. I have got to show them what's wrong with me.*

I gulp air down. I hold my breath. This time, it's going to be until I can feel my heart skip.

"WELL, IT LOOKS LIKE what we've got here is a possible case of periodic rapid heart action."

I'm in the exam room, fully clothed, sitting on the table, while they look at my test results, spread out over the exam counter.

"Does that mean we'll have to go in for open-heart? I mean seriously, Michael, I'm not opposed to it if we can really find out what's going on here. I've been reading up on a new pediatric valve syndrome, and I'm wondering if you could do a test just to rule that out."

My mother is now on a first-name basis with my cardiologist. They stand near each other when they consult. In an effort to clarify the confusing results of my latest monitor reading, he is personally explaining to her the odd fluctuations on my heart graphs.

"Oh, no, I don't think we're going to need that, Sandy. But what we really should do is some more tests under the close eye of hospital staff. Could we get Julie into hospital for a week and run a comprehensive assessment?"

"I don't think there's a problem in that. I'm just glad I've finally found someone who is actually competent enough to realize that this kid is sick. I'd say it's about time we were getting somewhere in this runaround, wouldn't you?"

"Absolutely."

THERE IS NOTHING MORE DISTINCTIVE than the smell of "hospital." As soon as the interior doors wisp open, you stand in shiny waxed hallways, the smell of canned breath, escaped from breathing tubes, wafts out from the rooms. The air is cool with a smack of oxygen that zings your nose if you breathe in too fast, and it's all mixed together with the clean fiber scent of bandages and sterile gauzes.

At the intake desk, they strap a little plastic band to my wrist, branded with my name in blurry blue dye like the stamp you see on rump roast.

MY MOTHER CHECKS ME IN. It's like vacation or going away to camp, which I've always wanted to do. I take the good blue suitcase, my best Paul Zindel books. I curl-iron my hair. I look nice. I count out nine pairs of underwear. I'm taking extra, just in case I get to stay.

My room is stocked with my very own welcome basket holding individual packs of Kleenex, a blue plastic bottle imprinted with the words "Keri Lotion," and a little tan swimming pool dish to throw up in. There's a swing-arm nightstand and a heavy curtain that clinks around the bed when somebody wants to do something that others shouldn't see. As soon as Mom leaves my room, I pull the curtain all the way back to the far corner of the bed, twist it into a skinny rope, and jam it tight behind the mattress.

I LOVE THE HOSPITAL. My bed goes up and down with a clicker. Jell-O awaits at my disposal. The nurses make their daily rounds, give me meds, take my temperature, ask about "bowel movements." And since I have no idea what they are and feel too stupid to ask, I guess at the right number from the expressions on their face.

They push a cart down the hallway and deliver and take away my food tray. They peel off the cling wrap and the locked-in aroma of warm mash—delicious and piping hot—steams my face. They joke about my taste for hospital food as I ravage the compartments of my plate; canned green beans, meat loaf, I don't care, I scarf it down.

Late mornings they come get me, lift me into a wheel-chair, and roll me down to a treadmill to count my heart-beats. I have no idea why they insist I ride in a chair. An aide scoops me out of my clean white nest and folds my feet into slippers. Why be wheeled when you can walk? But the care and kindness make me want to cry. And I want to stay as long as I can. In a few days, I will be de-pressing my call button like Dad on his remote, huffing "Where's my second fruit cup?"

They roll me down to the heart unit and park me by the station where the nurse works with her needles and gauges. It's a vast, open room, with a gym treadmill, blood pressure machines, EKG equipment, wires, and contraptions, all designed to hear the heart.

She hooks the familiar little pads to my chest and plugs the other ends into the machine. They clasp their fingers around my wrists and steady my elbows, helping me from wheelchair to treadmill. A belt gets locked around my waist and is affixed to the rails of the equip-ment, in case I collapse. After even a minute, I'm winded. But I'm getting stronger. Day by day, I walk faster and longer and the nurses are so impressed they say I might even get to go home early. Wouldn't that be nice?

And that's when I collapse. As long as my legs buckle at will, I get to stay: with my second helpings, with my stacks of books, and with my mother only a slow-fading memory.

MOM IS THERE, OF COURSE, every day, all day. From the time visiting hours begin to the moment they're over. But she is not with me. She visits other patients or con-

My beautiful mother in her stunt riding days, before she married Dad and had me.

By the time I was five, Mom and Grandma were racing me to the hospital after suspected food poisonings.

When I was three, Grandma Madge used to take me fishing. Then we'd climb in the car and go off and get in a wreck.

It was usually after Mom slipped the littl white pill under my tongue that my migr got worse.

My little brother Danny was the cutest and healthiest thing that had ever come out of the Gregory family.

We mostly stayed home on our dead-end dirt road, and there was a great gulf between how we really were and how we looked when we got out.

Mom had over a hundred pairs of shoes waiting for the dates, dinner and couples events my father woul someday take her to.

What really happened that Christmas morning: Mom screeching through the trailer, threatening to commit suicide.

Dad was summoned with a set of decent clothes only when a demonstration of fatherly support was paramount at a hospital.

The foster kids always wanted so desperately to fit into the picture.

Mom posed me as a model and carried the Polaroids in her purse in case she ran into a "nice older man" who wanted to have a look at me.

All that remained our six-bedroom double-wide mans was a deserted, smoldering footba field of twisted me

Summer weekends after I left home, I'd drive down to the new trailer and Danny would bound out and fling his arms around me.

Me with my 4-H horse, Skipster's Barr.

Our last Ohio photograph, taken on Mother's Day. Two months later, I would learn about Munchausen by proxy and start to rebuild a life out of the ashes.

Will Shivley

Alone in my house of mirrors, I saw the image
my mother had created in my mind's eye: a sickly
creature, destined to die early.

Two of the toughest kids in Ohio, tearing along an empty highway, singing lyrics of a lost childhood without smile or irony.

I am a real woman now. I have lived a lot of life. I know what it feels like to be cut, caged, or taken, and I know what it feels like to escape.

sults with the staff at the nurses' station. When she stops by my room at night to pick up her purse, she slips me a scrap of paper with the room numbers of the kids she visited, kids in for cancer, for tests, for operations.

"Here, Sis, why don't you go up there to the surgery floor and visit room six-twelve? She's the sweetest little girl, about your age, and she's getting a brain tumor taken out on Friday. They're not sure if she's going to make it; it would be so nice for her to get cheered up by you, honey."

I'll go anywhere in the hospital Mom tells me to, as long as it's not home. My family members are as remote as white fluffy clouds that have floated away in my sky and I am like the great god Odin, from the Douglas Adams books I'm reading, whose life's luxury is spent slipped between crisp linen sheets, surrounded by the pampering care of people who work in shifts to fulfill my basic needs. A delicious return to infancy. My books and my sheets and those little compartments full of food are all I need.

When Mom comes in, she reads my chart on the door and paces around the room, hoping to catch my doctor.

I bury myself in a book, hoping she'll leave.

"You being good for them, Sis?"

"Uh-huh."

"Well, we are all so very lucky to be in here with Michael as our cardiologist. This is the chance of a life-time, to have them do all these tests. We're bending over backwards to get you the best of care, you know? So for God's sake, Julie, don't fuck it up, let them do whatever they need to do and let's get to the bottom of this thing."

THE TIMES I'M SCARED are when a throng of boys with stethoscopes and white coats whisk into my room unannounced with a doctor leading the way. These are medical students. The doctor pontificates on palpitations, prolapses, and murmurs, while the students fan around my bed to stare at the thirteen-year-old patient, a rarity in this predominately geriatric field.

He reaches behind my neck with fingers soft and distracted, and unties my gown. The thin-washed cotton peels softly down my chest, settling into a flimsy loose roll around my waist. He flutters his fingertips along me, still lecturing to the students, feeling for ticks and skips. Fat tears swell in my eyes and one by one plunge over the rim, tears so heavy that they trickle to my collarbones. *Don't fuck it up, Julie, let them do whatever they want.* He instructs the students to feel, too, and cold, strange digits finger their way toward me, pressing, holding, and floating faintly like ghosts around the heart-related stops on my chest.

To feel the beat of my heart those hands have to get oriented. They graze against the tiny bottom swell of my almost-there breast; a valiant effort of minuscule curve trying to grow out of my ill health like a fragile flower on a craggy ledge. They push up into a rib, climb up on top of my nipple and, while tears fall harder, press in on the virgin center, never touched before, trying to catch the rhythm of my heart faintly beating.

They touch me without breaking stride in their talk to notice. I am just a girl, a girl men touch without asking, a girl men disrobe without even seeing her tears. Then, as fast as they swarmed in, they're gone, turning like a school of fish, a precision drill team of white coats leaving me to cover up and rub the singe of foreign fingers from my skin.

MY STAY IS ALMOST OVER. I am going to have to go home eventually. I have done all the tests. I have worn another heart monitor, done more EKGs, worked up to a feeble jog on the treadmill. I have visited the girl in 612.

A NURSE WALKS INTO MY ROOM for night check. She picks up the unused throw-up dish off my swivel arm table.

"So, how you doin', hon?" She walks to the sink.

"Fine."

"Liking the food?" She runs the tap and starts filling the tub with water.

"Yeah, it's good."

"Ready to go home?"

"Kinda."

"Awww, you miss your family, don't you?" She sits on the side of my bed and pulls a razor from the pocket of her white smock. I bolt up, eyes wide.

"We're going to have to shave you now, honey."

"Shave me?" My chest could not possibly have any more hair on it.

"Down *here*." She pats for my pubic bone under the thin hospital blanket.

"What? I'm done, I'm going home! I don't have anything down there!" I jerk my knees up. "I'm here for my heart!"

"Well, honey, we can't have any hair down there because even just a little bit would be in the doctor's way. That's where he cuts with his scalpel."

"What scalpel?"

"That's the knife he uses for the test."

My eyes widen.

"For your heart catheterization." I'm trying her patience. Why do I have to make her job harder? My mother is here all day, every day, surely I know.

"That's the reason you're here this week, so they can figure out what's happening in the valves of your heart. Tomorrow they're going to make a little incision in the vein of your arm and the artery of your thigh and run some electrical connectors into the valves so they can see it on a TV screen. You might think it's kinda neat, watching your heart on TV."

This has got to be a mistake. Maybe this nurse got a slip of paper from my mom for somebody else. It's a mix-up. My eyes are searching my bedspread, as fast as my brain is scanning. How did this happen? They're going to cut me. My breath quickens, my eyes fixate in horror.

"You, you can't do this to me," my voice speaks by itself. "You can't do it," it says louder, "my mother is making it up!"

I can't believe I blurted that out. I cannot believe I just said that! I jump to the back corner of the bed, clutching the covers up to my neck with one hand, slipping my other behind me, to pin that curtain to the headboard.

The nurse watches me hard. Her expression says she doesn't believe me. Maybe I don't believe me, either. I can't really believe I just said that. That would be ridiculous. My mother loves me. There's something wrong with me. I do feel sick. I am tired all the time. I am sick or else I wouldn't be here. If I wasn't sick the doctors wouldn't keep trying to fix me.

But still we stare. Nurse and I, frozen in eye lock. She is peering into me, the caged animal, trying to discern if I'm up to something or not. I stare back, afraid to take my eyes off her for even a second. She is scanning my face, probing behind my tears, for the glint that says *ha, ha, I'm joking,* for even the hint of smile that will crack open my mouth, and then we'll both have a good pressure-releasing laugh.

She doesn't find it.

"Be back in a sec." She sets the pan of water down without a sound. "Let me see what's going on." She pads out.

I am saved. They'll find out. They'll keep me. Mom'll be furious. I don't care. I can run away. I'll get a job. I can find a new family. I can go live with my cardiologist.

I think about the last time I sat in the doctor's office with my mother; how pissed she was when they couldn't find anything and how thrilled she was when they said I could go in the hospital. It was in my head even as I said to her, "See, we knew there was something wrong with me all along." Long-due answers on my illness were cause for celebration; I was relieved that the doctors finally believed her. But didn't I have a flash that I might be just agreeing because I was scared not to? Because I was stupid, because I failed in school, because I drooled? Didn't I think that maybe I was acting sicker because she slammed my head against the inside of the window on the way home if I didn't show them how sick I was? I tried to think straight. It made no sense. It was insane.

Mom knows what she's doing. She's the one who sees my symptoms.

The quiet of the hall fills with the hurried squeak of a single pair of nurse shoes.

My nurse forks over a pleated paper cup. "Take this. We're going to give it a few minutes."

She yanks the curtain from behind the mattress and flies it around the bed in one fluid motion. I throw my head into my hands and scream. My chest heaves like a baby, tears running down my face. *She's going to shave me.* The pills start to wash over me in a slow gradual tide. I fall into my bed and a corner of *Are You There, God? It's Me, Margaret* pokes me in the back. I throw my arm over my face, bite into the pad of flesh on my palm and sob bitterly as she lifts my gown. Cool air hits my bare skin, protected and warm, and she starts to lather. The place I promised myself nobody would ever touch. She pries my knees apart and runs the razor over me. I howl. I bite into my arm, past the IV holes and the bruises on my veins, the black sticky tape marks and the Band-Aided cotton ball, smeared with a single drop of blood. I cannot stand her hands on me. I hate my wet skin, the sick smell of my father's shave cream. There is not enough shaving cream between us so that our skin never touches. There could never be enough.

"Now, see, that wasn't so bad now, was it?"

THE NEXT MORNING THEY JOSTLE ME deep from within the arms of the mistress of sleep. Stink Pup's rat tail thumps a tap, tap against the inside of my arm. My head turns dreamily to see him, oh wait, it's two fingers tapping for a vein. Drip, drip, the IV goes, it runs into the bruise, spreads warm through my vein. I turn my head again, the drug trickles through every tiny blood vessel in my neck, creating countless delicious rivulets flowing into me.

Two men have me on a sheet, sliding me on nothing, from bed to gurney. There's a stick in me somewhere, a pinch, hazy and soft, so far away. Did I step on a wasp? Was that me dripping wet from the pool running over the grass and stepping on the electric fence, the gate left down, strung across the yard, my glassy foot glued to the shocking grass? No, it's only my big toe, toasty from under the covers, hitting the cold metal bar. I can sleep now, they tell me, I am safe in the hospital. *Ca-clunk,* they snap the guardrails up. There is no gravity, just suspension in a nothing world. I'm living on the white, empty ceiling I have always wanted.

We are rolling down the hall. I am rolling through the nothing world, warm and tucked in tight like the sheets on the spare-room mattress at Grandma's house. You'd have to kick your legs wildly to get free, but who wants to make the effort?

In the halls, dust specks float in dappled sunlight, warm fizz of flat cola, swaying in the window of a back corner last-row seat, a voice in geography floats through the air, menacing a test on Friday, lulling me into cardiac rest. I'd give all my money, all my stolen lunch money, just to sleep in the sun. To lay my head against a warm glass window and feel an angel's breath, hot on my scalp. We turn a corner, the wheels sliding spin on the waxed white tile floor. Take me away, make me sleep, my lids cannot bear the weight.

"JULIE, JULIE, HONEY." It's Mom, bending over me, looking bright into my drugged eyes. She is hoping for the best. She knows I'm in good hands. She waves to me in bon voyage fashion.

My father stands solid, his chest puffed out, arms stiff at his sides like a gingerbread man, big beaver grin on his face. "Good luck, Sissy. We love you." I think I see his bottom eyelid quiver with a brimming tear. His forehead is lined into thick vertical folds. I raise my leaden fingers to squeeze one. They look like the 3-D mountain ranges from my globe in fourth grade—the one I used to study with my hands when all the world lay at my fingers. I want to touch the mountains that run across my father's forehead. My hand stretches out for my dad but they wheel me on.

They park me in the operating room, bustle around me.

"Breathe deep, Julie." The voice from above lowers a mask over my nose and mouth.

I breathe as they tell me and slip down elevator shafts. Ebony's tail is a burr loaf and thumps like a club on the porch. Stink Pup's snarl-grin lifts his upper lip while the fishhook dangles out of it. Ebony pushes her nose under my hand and bump, bumps it up. *Okay, I'll pat your head.* Ebony's tongue, lick, lick, on the back of my hand. *Oh, babydog. I love you, too.* Or is that the needle stick of another IV? And Ebony's nose under my palm—is that really her or just a stranger's hand, trying to steady mine?

I MAKE A DOUBLE CHIN, drawing my head down to watch. They pull my right arm out and flip it over. The crook of my forearm is sliced neatly with a scalpel and filleted open like a chicken breast. It is a bloodless act. The electrical wire snakes into my vein. They push it up, up my arm, down over my shoulder and into my heart. I feel nothing but the slightest tingle. We have contact. The crew points me to the screen so I can watch my heart beat on TV. *Don't forget to tell him you've got sharp chest pains when you breathe.*

My eyes blink. The screen shows a lump of heart, beating in two little pumps at a time. *Ba-bump, ba-bump.* Surely this is not me. Not my body.

"Idz like a soap opra," I slur. The crew chuckles, I am in this with them, and I feel good that I can get older people to laugh.

The doctor stands at the bottom of the table and I lie there, pelvic bones poking through thin white sheets. He studies his tray of many scalpels.

What did I say last night? He selects his knife. *C'mon, Julie, be a good patient, don't fuck it up.* He pulls my limp right leg out from under the sheet and kinks my thigh up and out for maximum arch, like he was getting ready to crack a giant crab leg.

I watch.

He slides his blade across my taut muscle like a bow to a violin. *Please don't do this to me.* He has broken the seal of my body. Blood flows from the slit and rushes; staining, screaming across the cool white sheet. *My mother is making it up.* I flop my head side to side, panting. *Please don't do this to me.* I look down; blood flows out of me, red races across a field of white. Is this me? My leg? My blood? The doctor threads his wire toward the incision in my thigh. *My mother is making it up.* My legs are moving, curling away. Don't let it touch me, get the wire out, get it out! *What happened to you? You were being such a good patient.* I'm struggling to my lazy elbows. They fold like cheap cards. My arm wire jerks with me. I have to see, the cut on my thigh, I have to watch the wire go in, to know it is real. I pant like a woman in labor. *Where am I?* I pivot my head in slow motion, scanning the startled faces of those who cannot hold me down, just a sweet complacent thing, me the good patient.

The doctor halts his wire, staring calmly into my eyes from behind his mask. *Quick, get her sedated, she's ruining the test.* I cannot see his lips move, but I hear the words. They scurry with their breathing tube; scrape it up my nose, snake it down my throat, tie up my other arm, tap wildly for a vein not yet collapsed.

Stick. Injection. Sedation. Calm. Enough to last me another twelve years.

M Y FIRST DAY BACK TO SCHOOL is a mess. My new friends are ecstatic I'm out of the hospital. I am despondent for the same reason. At lunch, I walk into the cafeteria with Missy and . . . Surprise . . . a welcome-back party with Twinkies, King Dons, Swiss Rolls, and pizza. I put on the smile but I am dying inside, dying to tell them. I hold back my tears until they rush forth and my girlfriends uncomfortably dismiss themselves, one by one, miffed that I am crying at their party.

The only one left is Missy, arm around me, trying to get it out. *What's wrong, is there something wrong with your heart, are you going to die?* We dissolve into the sea of orange and yellow lockers and I tell her between sniffles some of my confusion. Missy is speechless. The bells are ringing. She'll write me later, she says, and she vanishes, weaving through the lockers and out of sight.

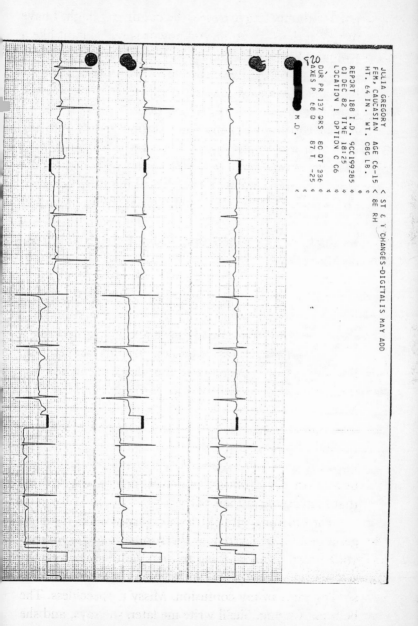

JULIA GREGORY   < ST & T CHANGES-DIGITALIS MAY ADD
FEM, CAUCASIAN   AGE 06-15   < 8E RH
HT. 64 IN.   WT. C8C LB.   *
                                    *
REPORT 188 I.D. 9CC199285   *
CI DEC 82 TIME 18:25   *
LOCATION 1 OPTION C C6   *

520
DUR PR 137 QRS   80 QT 336   *
AXES P 68 Q   87 T -25   *
M.D.

HOSPITAL
PREOPERATIVE CHECKLIST

Date _____ 12/3/82 _____

Procedure _____ Cath _____

EVENING BEFORE SURGERY

Ward Clerk Responsibilities:
-Voucher Card Packet on chart .... yes ()✓
-Initial Postop order sheets
 in front of chart .... yes ()✓
-All order sheets in back of
 chart .... yes ()✓
-Disposition form signed .... yes () n/a()✓
-Type and crossmatch drawn .... yes () n/a()✓
-Chest x-rays done .... yes ()✓
-Additional x-rays done .... yes () n/a()✓
-EKG done .... yes ()✓
-Consent signed and witnessed ...... yes ()✓

_____ 12/2/82
Ward Clerk Signature   Date

MORNING OF SURGERY

-Embosser plate on chart .... yes ()
-Preop urinalysis and blood
 results on chart .... yes ()
-Preop x-rays report on chart ...... yes ()
-EKG strip on chart .... yes ()

_____ _____
Ward Clerk Signature   Date

Comments: _____
_____
_____
_____
_____

_____ _____
Ward Clerk Signature   Date

Pharmacy Technician:
-Preop medications administered

Date _____ Time _____

_____
Pharmacy Technician Signature

1/81

MORNING OF SURGERY

Professional Nurse Responsibilities
-Temperature _98°_ Pulse _20_
-Respiration _55_ Blood Pressure
-Weight _90#_
-Allergies   yes() n
 Specify _IVP DYE_
-ID Band on Patient   yes()
-Consent signed and
 witnessed   yes()✓
-Isolation precautions   yes() n
 If yes, type
-Danger List patient   yes() n
-Voided yes() time _6:30_
-Wearing hospital gown
 only   yes() r
 If no, explain
-Elastic stockings   yes() r
-Wig removed   yes() r
-Glasses removed   yes() r
-Contact lenses removed   yes() r
-Hearing aid removed   yes() r
-Prosthetic device
 removed   yes() r
-Dentures removed   yes() ✻
-All cosmetics removed   yes() ✻
-All jewelry removed   yes() ✻
-All items removed from
 hair   yes() ✻
-All nail polish removed   yes() ✻

Comments: _____

Specific Patient Considerations

Pt very Emotional + Fear

of test.

Directions: All responsibiliti
            must be completed
            to signature of RN
            and before patient
            departure to OR.

                            12
_____
RN/GN Signature   Da

The rest of the day my other friends are cool to me. In fifth period history I am passed the note. Missy's fat script letters pen out: "We know you made the whole thing up, trying to get us to feel sorry for you. It won't work. Nobody's mom does those things and we hate you for lying. You are scumbucket trash. We want nothing to do with you." Scratched at the bottom are all ten of my girlfriends' names.

HEART SURGERY, IODINE INJECTIONS, tubes shoved, slits sliced, blood drawn. These things change a kid. At the cellular level. You forget what you were like before they cut you, before they shaved you. The past drifts away; inaccessible. You only look to the future when they'll find what's wrong so it can all be over; the tests, the trying, the meds you swallow without knowing why.

At home, a kitchen cabinet has been cleared for my medication. Where food used to be is now a cupboard full of Julie food: meds, weight-gain wafers, and six-packs of chocolatey Ensure Plus, the canned supplement drink they gave me in the hospital to complement my brimming meals.

Mom says I may be allergic to regular food, but I can drink as much Ensure Plus as I want. One little can is like eating an entire three-course meal. There's no difference, she says, absolutely none.

December 15, 1982

M.D.

RE: Julia Gregory

Dear Dr. ▇▇▇

As mentioned to you on the telephone, we had the pleasure of having Ms. Julia Gregory on our Cardiology Service between December 1, 1982 and her discharge on the evening of December 6, 1982. We were most impressed with her history of periodic rapid heart action, and we reviewed carefully her previously completed Holter Monitor showing a number of episodes of supraventricular tachycardia with periods of "warm-up" and "slow down" plus secondary T-wave changes.

Her physical examination was remarkable in terms of her asthenic habitus, joint laxity, and general Marfanoid appearance. More remarkable than that was her postural tachycardia, many occasions consisting of supine heart rates of 70 rising to as high as 140 upon standing. She variously had a mid systolic click, but never a murmur and not a distinctive examination for mitral valve prolapse. We recognised her previously negative echo in terms of prolapse.

Her electrocardiogram was of special interest in terms of her borderline short PR interval, and the suggestion that she had Delta waves in anterior precordial leads.

We did complete electrophysiologic testing and found her totally normal without evidence of Wolff-Parkinson-White or other forms of pre-excitation. She had no underlying, no induceable dysrhythmia either supraventricular or ventricular in nature.

We completed an exercise nuclear angiographic study demonstrating no provocable dysrhythmia and excellent exercise tolerance as well as normal ventricular contractility. We demonstrated normal thyroid function tests, normal VMA in a 24 hour urine specimen, normal 5-HIAA, also in a 24 hour urine specimen, and a normal response to ACTH testing. We also measured her plasma volume and found it to be normal, (41cc's/kgm) this excluding volume depletion as the cause of her postural tachycardia.

As mentioned to you on the telephone, we therefore felt we had defined the syndrome of dysautonomia most often responsible for the postural tachycardia syndrome and usually seen in prolapse patients. In my own mind, I think she has "pre-prolapse", and by this I mean that by the time she is 18 or this will be manifest as a more distinctive auscultitory exam, etc.

the time being, she certainly doesn't need endocarditis prophylaxis,
I believe her treatment should include the following:

1. No activity restriction.
2. Salt liberalization.
3. Periodic Atenolol in low doses, (25 to 50mg., per day), this designed
   to blunt the effect of hyperactive beta receptors. The latter of
   course is a presumptive diagnosis, but I believe the most appropriate
   one in her regard at this time.

will have sought suture removal in your office, and she expects to return
for follow-up as you requested in January of 1983. I will be very pleased
continue to follow this patient, and I discussed this in considerable
il with both the patient and both parents.

k you very much for allowing us to see this most fascinating patient. A
of the electrophysiologic study will be forwarded to you upon its completion,
ill a copy of the hospital discharge summary when typed.

se call at any time if there should be further developments.

erely,

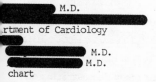

M.D.

rtment of Cardiology

M.D.
M.D.
chart

SWALLOWED. HOOK, LINE, AND SINKER.

WE STAND IN THE CORRIDOR of Ohio State Hospital, me, Mom, and my cardiologist. Sometimes teens are just tired and run-down, he says. I don't have a heart murmur, he says. And he can't really do any more for me.

Mom talks in soft confidence like a colleague. She leans in close, just like old times. She's considering the tests they've been through together and pondering the disappointing outcome of this one.

"Hmmm. Well, Michael. Let's get a plan of attack together here. In the face of these inconclusive test results, now is the time that I think we really need to move in with the open-heart surgery and finally, once and for all, get to the bottom of this thing."

He stares at her.

"Ms. Gregory, Julie does not need heart surgery. I'm sure you're pleased to hear that." He clears his throat. "There is nothing in these tests that leads me to believe that she would benefit from such an invasive procedure. I believe, in time, her heart condition will clarify and become more pronounced so we can assess it, or she may just outgrow it on her own. At most, we could consider her a possible candidate for an early precondition of mitral valve prolapse."

"You're kidding me."

"No, I'm not. Julie is within normal range of our tests."

"I can't believe it! I cannot believe this! You're not going to dig into this and do the open-heart? I thought we had agreed to follow this through to the end,

Michael. I thought you said you were committed to me on this."

"I'm committed to finding Julie's illness, Ms. Gregory, but Julie doesn't need heart surgery. Usually parents are thrilled to—"

"Oh, that's just it? That's all you're going to do? Just drop me like a hot potato? I mean, for crying out loud, why can't I just have a normal kid like other mothers? I mean I'm a good mom, 4-H, horses, swimming pool, camping trips. I do and do and do. You act like I'm doing something wrong. What did I do to deserve *this*?" She thrusts an arm back to me.

I'm standing behind my mother's left leg, my eyes glued to the doctor, boring an SOS into his eyes: *Don't make me go, don't let her take me.*

"Ms. Gregory, I didn't say you weren't a good mother. But I can't do anything else here. You need to drop the heart procedures. Period." And with that he turned on his heel.

"Well, you're the one who's going to be sorry," Mom screeches, "when this kid dies on you. That's what. 'Cause you're going to get sued out the ying-yang for being such an incompetent idiot. Can't even find out what's wrong with a thirteen-year-old girl! You are insane! This kid is sick, you hear me? She's sick!"

GOOD MORNING, DR. STRONG'S OFFICE."
"Hello, I'm a new patient looking for a cardiologist. Well, actually it's for my teen daughter. You see, she's got mitral valve prolapse, and I'm scared to death it's getting worse."

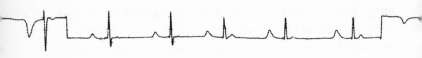

A COUNTRY SUMMER IN OHIO is just about one of the lushest, sexiest things you could ask for. It makes any girl want to traipse around in cutoff Daisy Duke shorts and a bikini top. Greenery gone berserk, vining all over everything, pregnant with shoots or seeds just bursting out of every split-open pod and juicy stalk; bullfrogs sit down at the pond and beat their hearts out at night in sexual frustration until the air sirens with a frenzy that gives and pulls, escalates in passion and dies down again to bare silence. It is delicious.

I sit on the back porch hot and restless for action, the action where a boy looks at you and you get dizzy with the excitement that he might like you, all the while trying not to look back. I sit on the back porch, restless and bored, and pick the ticks off of Stink Pup and Ebony. I do not kill bugs. The fat ones I collect on a paper plate with the hair and the scabs that tear off with them as the dog jerks its head back over its shoulder in an annoyed, watch-it sort of way. When I have four or five big ones on the plate, their legs waving wildly in the air, I pad across the soft grass to the pasture and dump them in a bush on the edge of the woods. They are just trying to live. Why should I step on them so they explode blood, or burn them with a match? I don't know why they are here but that doesn't mean they don't belong. The small ones I toss in the grass and they crawl away, sometimes trucking like hell back toward the dog, but that will just give me something to do another night.

Tick ranching, this is what my hot teenage nights have come to. While other kids my age are necking in cars, pretending to talk for hours just in order to kiss minutes before curfew, or out at movies with their best friend and his older brother, shrieking breathless in the front seat of his Camaro as they roar around corners, I am sitting here on a dead-end dirt road, cultivating ticks from the burr-crusted coats of a couple of farm hounds.

Now that I'm in ninth grade and Dr. Strong has me on medication for mitral valve prolapse, Mom wants to get something done about my mouth hanging open all the time.

"It makes you look like a nigger, Julie. Jesus, close your lips and breathe right!"

That winter, we see an ear, nose, and throat specialist in Columbus. Since my heart catheterization forced Mom to come into the University Hospital every day on her own, she's felt better about expanding our search into the center of the city. We got this close here, so there's a good chance we can get the rest of me solved.

Mom and the doctor talk about nasal passages and

how the lack of air flowing through them can cause all sorts of medical problems, from heart irregularities to restricted oxygen traveling to the brain.

I sit on the doctor's exam table and his face moves in close. I can feel his warm breath drift across my bottom lip. Huhh. Huhh. Tilting my chin up, he sticks a pointy light in my nostril and spreads my nose all around with his finger. He says "Wellll" and "I seeee."

They schedule me for a same-day procedure, where he'll go in and chisel the extra cartilage from my nasal passages in the hope that I can close my lips and breathe normally. He says I've got a deviated septum.

The office where he explains my operation has deep comfy chairs, their designer upholstery cut from chenille. Before-and-after profiles of other people with deviated septums hang framed behind him, spanning the length of his office wall. I look closely while they talk, wondering if anyone else has noticed that each nose my doctor has fixed looks different after he operates. I thought I might ask him but he and Mom are holding direct eye contact. He leans across his mahogany table toward her, she leans from her chenille chair toward him, between them is an X ray of my nose, crowded with cartilage. Mom uses her finger like a magic wand. "Could you shave that little Roman bump off and give her a ski slope there at the bottom?"

The doctor leans back and smiles. "We can do whatever you like, Sandy."

Mom tells me this procedure is going to count as one of my Christmas presents because it's not fully covered by insurance. But it's worth it, she says. Not only will my doctor make me breathe better, but he's also going to make me beautiful.

THE NOSE IS NOT A PART of the body designed to wear a cast. But they have plastered my nose, what's left of it, and anchored it firmly to my face with thin white strips of medical tape. The pain is excruciating. My cartilage has been shaved, the tip of my nose nipped and tucked. The first couple days my eyes are black and blue and swollen shut and I must hold my head very, very still. Blood and mucus cake around my nostrils, a snot bubble blows when I breathe out. I am not allowed anywhere for two weeks, so I stay home from school and can take my time wheelbarrowing bales of hay to the horses, hauling in buckets of coal, and chopping wood for the stove. I'm moving slow, because my sinus plates feel like they've been shattered with a mallet. The pressure never ceases, just a constant broken feeling in my face, like chips of fine china or slivers of a bird's delicate bone, broken in its wing.

They say I can't wear sunglasses for six weeks: My nose is so fragile that even the slightest weight could collapse its new shape. The pain in my face is all I can feel. I cannot remember a time without it, I can't imagine a time free of it. It's all I can see before me, a sea of pain, with me adrift in the middle, clutching a log, trying not to go under. They can do anything they want now. Because I know, deep down, I'll never get better.

"HAS HE TOUCHED YOU, you know, *privately?*"

Mom had me trapped on the bed for one of her talks.

"No."

And it was true. I loved Dad; he never did anything bad to me. I didn't like to be in a swimsuit around him, but he never did anything that I could say for sure was wrong.

"Well, Penny told someone that Dan was, you know, and they believed it. That goddamned mother-fucking son of a bitch—I know he did it, so help me God I'd like to see someone take a gun and blow his brains out—but the caseworker's gonna come down, maybe take Penny and probably ask some questions, and you just answer no, okay?"

"Okay."

"Tell them your dad would never do anything like that."

But when I came in from outside the next day, Mom had Penny, one of the original foster kids, in the living room, her beautiful blond hair wrapped round and round Mom's hand.

"You little slut. How dare you make up that shit when I'm your mother and you never had it so good? I gave you a horse and let you be in 4-H and bought you clothes and took you to the fair and . . ."

I slipped into my room but I could hear Penny trying to tell Mom, through tears, that she wasn't making it up. Dad did pull out his magazines in the garage. She was sorry, Mom, she didn't mean to tell. Her voice went in and out, like her head was being rammed into the couch, the wall, the hutch.

I had an ear down at the bottom crack of my door, my heart racing.

"You slut, you make me sick. I hope they rape you where they take you, then you'll know what it's really like."

The next day she was gone.

WHEN THE FOSTER KIDS FIRST CAME, I used to have to beat them. In the beginning, I felt like I was in some special elite group. They were the outsiders. I was the real kid who counted. They were pseudochildren, ghost kids. They were just there to give us money to keep building on.

They came into our house and we were just supposed to automatically be brothers and sisters. Most of them were kicking and crying, screaming that their real mom was coming to get them as soon as she could find them.

They were foreigners under our roof and stranger than the old men. At least the vets had their own separate wing of the trailer that Mom locked up. She put them away because it was against the law to have both foster kids and war veterans. So when the caseworker came to check on things, Dad would load up the old men in the wagon and go out for a while. Then, when the VA caseworker came in, he'd take the kids out on a drive.

We lived not even remembering that the old men were under our own roof, they were so removed. But the foster kids shared our rooms, our closets, our toys, our clothes, our bunk beds, and our mom and dad.

Mom puts the flyswatter in my hand and shows me how to do it. Grab their wrist and whack the hard plastic handle over their pink baby palms. She stands in the doorway of their room until I can crack hard enough to make them scream. Some of them are only a year or so younger than me.

It was just us then, me and Mom, bosom buddies. When we went shopping after doctors' appointments, we left the foster kids in the car. I was her best friend, and when she made fun of how stupid Lloyd was, the way he stuttered and had bowlegs from having rickets as a baby, I laughed right along with her jokes. When she pointed at fat Penny and told long-waisted Ricky how he was shaped funny, I did too, and we giggled like schoolgirls.

Mom shared all this with only me, and being let in on her private funnies was as warm a feeling as peeing in the pool when no one was watching. I beat the kids for Mom because I was still her little helper. God love me.

LLOYD WAS SUPPOSED TO GET IT one morning because he didn't pick up his room fast enough. Mom marched the flyswatter back to me and crammed it into my grip.

"I'll leave it to you, Sis. You give a holler if he gives you any trouble."

I stood in the doorway like a soldier, glaring at the boy. He stood stiff with his bowlegs, staring back from the side of the big round toy box, shaped to look like the blue earth, trying to drop the toys in as silently as he could. I was going to make him pay. I rushed forward and grabbed his little hand, flipped it over, and hit and hit. For a second there was no response. And then the air cracked with his scream. It came from a low, guttural place, as if his soul itself had been punctured and had unleashed its own cry of defense. The sound turned me nauseous. It sounded like torture. And I was the torturer.

I let go of him and took a few steps back. His bottom lip sucked in fast as he tried to stay breathing. His hand was streaked red, pulsing with the heated throb of welts rising. He couldn't take his eyes off me. I couldn't take my eyes off him. We stood there, staring, panting, four feet between us. Mom yelled out from the kitchen and we jumped in our skin from the jolt her voice sent straight through us. We still stared, eyes locked on to one another, and I took the flyswatter and hit my own hand while Lloyd let out the cries. We did it for Mom, we did it for us.

And after that, without ever acknowledging it, the foster kids and I just naturally fell into an advanced system of nonverbal communication. An entire sentence or potential danger could be boiled down to an essence flashed in a single split-second darting glance, a tiny, undetectable emphasis on a word, the brush of a finger along the kitchen counter.

These messages told us everything we needed to know about where Mom was, how she was feeling. We were psychic CBing. We were POW kids in a hideout tin trailer, and we began to look out for each other. The screams we heard were paralyzing at first, but they later mobilized us with a heroic panic to jump in and take it ourselves. It wasn't just that "other" kids were getting beaten, it was now our brothers and sisters. Stepping in became our own choice and was somehow easier to handle than standing passive.

And since I was the oldest and knew how to smooth her out the best, from all the times I hadn't shown the doctor how sick I really was, my skills were honed and polished. I alone could save the others from what I knew would kill them, in spirit at least.

I came to know every nuance of imbalance Mom careened to, every far corner she drifted into, every crevice she slipped through. I kept my antennas tuned for any outer stimulus that would throw her off. As the great shock absorber, I stood firm, invited the chaos on her screen into me, neutralized the waves, and adjusted the knobs in order to take the static out.

When I'd hear the cry from Lloyd's throat fill the trailer, I'd bound into the living room and say, "Mom. It was me. I lied. I'm the one who told Lloyd I'd clean the room and he could watch TV. I forgot. It's my fault. I'm sorry." The most direct, complete information, delivered in one condensed, easy-to-comprehend package. Sometimes she'd turn on me, and scrawny little brown-haired, bowlegged, stuttering Lloyd would slip, almost unnoticed, past the curve of the couch and go hide.

And soon it was me and Maria as the new bosom buddies. We could share a private funny about Mom with just our eyes alone—like the time Mom lost her hairpiece on a branch when we all went on a trail ride with the 4-H Club.

And within a few months, when Mom was beating Maria in the living room, I ran in to offer my own skull to the sharp heel bone of her hand—and got hit harder for having such a hard head that hurt her hand in the first place. When she was done, I stumbled off to the back bedroom, a closed-off addition, piled high with all the stuff we bought but never used.

Maria tiptoed through the tiny laundry room that led to the bedroom door and glanced over her shoulder to make sure Mom hadn't followed. She crept back to me in her stocking feet, weaving her way through paths cut in the junk. She found me crouched in the back corner and sank down the wall, draping her little arms around me and squeezing tight. She was not gonna let me go.

"I love you, Mom," she said.

"I love you, too, Maria."

IT WAS IN TENTH GRADE that I first heard the term "emancipated minor." Kids living on their own, working jobs to pay their bills, free from their parents! All you had to do was talk to the school counselor, sign some papers, and they'd help you get it set up. I was going to get out. And I was going to take Maria with me.

I made an appointment with Mr. Marks, our school's part-time counselor. I calmly, rationally explained what I needed and sat with pen in hand, ready to sign.

"Well, why do you want to leave home?"

I wasn't prepared for that. I didn't think I'd have to tell him why. I ventured out a few things and he raised his eyebrows.

He said he'd think on it and call me back to his office when he came up with something. But who he called instead was Mom and Dad.

That night in the kitchen Mom caught me by the hair and slung me to the floor. Dad grabbed both angles of the countertop for leverage and, hauling his leg back again and again, sank steel-toed boots into the hollow of my belly.

For the rest of sophomore year, Mr. Marks took me out of art class every week to counsel me for an overactive imagination.

MOM AND I SIT in the intestinal exploration wing of a new medical center. Two nurses prepare a separate cubicle for me, so I can drink the barium meal in private. The other nurse stands at the sink, mixing up the gunk that will light up my intestines.

"So where you guys from? Do you live here in Lancaster?"

"We're right on the Fairfield-Hocking line, just about forty minutes away, to the southwest of Lancaster."

"Julie, what flavor would you like to choose, hon? Yep, you get a choice. Orange, chocolate, or strawberry." The nurse turns back to Mom. "Murray, that's my hubby, and I live down out toward Pataskala, so you're not far from us at all. Do you play bridge?"

"Oh, we love it. Julie, answer her, now, what flavor do you want?"

"Which one tastes best?"

"Well, they all taste prit-tee bad. But if I had to pick one, I'd take the orange, it tastes like Orange Crush."

I okay it.

She mixes the flavor into the bottle. "We've got a little group that meets every week for a game," she turns back from the sink and winks at Mom, "without the boys. Just us girls."

"Well, you ought to come down to our house for a bridge night. Maybe we can get a team of nurses together, or at least, you know, get away from the men." Mom starts to squirm. "I'd love to have you down to the farm. We've got sixteen beautiful acres of woods and pastures around us. It's just beautiful."

"Ahh, I bet that is pretty. Well, I think we might just do that sometime. Now, Ms. Gregory, you'll have to sit in the room with Julie and make sure she drinks all of this, so we can get an X ray of the lower intestine."

The nurse smiles at us, hands me the drink, and walks out the doorway.

Mom leans after her. "Thank you so much, and make sure you jot down your phone number for me before we leave." She turns back to me, "All right, let's go, Sis. Let's get this done and over with."

I touch the metal malt container of thick barium to my mouth. It's orange chalk, ground up into a quart of oil, mixed in a base of magnet dust. After gulping down a mouthful, the most natural response to barium is to vomit it out as far from your body as possible.

A memory of metal washes over me. What was it now, the zolt of red match tips sinking into my tongue? Why am I still at the hospital? What are they looking for? Is my stomach messed up? I look at Mom. *Help me, please, help me.* Tears stream down my face. I choke down the barium, belch it back up; sour, thick bubbles. *Let's get this over with, Sis.* My throat flexes open, pinches shut. *Please, help me, Mom, don't make me drink this.*

But Mom's gaze is fixed in midair. She looks right through me, mouthing imaginary conversation. A muscle in her jaw tweaks with a rapid pulse and her animated eyes dance over the scene before her, the only one she can see as she stares into my face. It's not me here, crying, trying to force down a barium meal. It's not the exam room where we sit in the medical center. She's smiling at the circle of nurses fanned around the good dining table in our bay-windowed addition, munching out of a party box of potato chips, playing bridge, laughing over husbands, late into the night, just the girls.

ROENTGEN FINDINGS

Upper GI series with small bowel study. With ingestion of th
barium, it flows freely through the esophagus into the stomac
No hiatal hernia is demonstrated. The gastric mucosa is nor
The duodenal bulb and loop are normal.

With ingestion of a secondglass of barium, serial films of the
small bowel were taken. These demonstrate an entirely normal
small bowel mucosal pattern, as well as a normal appearing te
ileum. No evidence of any separation of dilatation of loops
seen.

Impression. 1. Normal Upper GI series.
             2. Normal small bowel study.

X - RAY REPORT   COLUMBUS

M Y PROJECT FOR 4-H was a registered quarter horse named Skipster's Barr. Barr stood fifteen hands at the withers—towering over me—magnificent and regal with his sleek brown coat, gleaming muscles, and four white socks.

Barr was supposed to be a barrel racer, with record timing in the ring for the barrel-racing contests Mom wanted to enter me in. But she said he turned out to be just as lazy as I was.

It was my secret relief to have an uncooperative horse. The thought of steering a high-strung, adrenaline-amped equine around hairpin barrel turns was enough to make me nauseous. At least now I had an excuse. But we hooked up a box spring to the riding mower, piled on cinder blocks, and drug a practice ring in the field anyway, and Mom'd haul Barr out to it to show me how it was done from her trick-riding days. She'd spring up in the saddle with a rallying *Yeeeee-haaaa,* crack the whip over my horse's beautiful rump, and gouge her spurs into his ribs until he ran so fast he nearly scraped her off around the barrels.

By the time they screeched to a halt in front of me, Barr's nostrils were slinging snot and his soft eyes were flared with terror.

But on summer days when Mom was busy in her closet or in a good mood, I'd tell her I wanted to take Barr to the upper fields to practice running him. I'd have to kick and kick and kick with my heels just to get him to trot off the farm as fast as possible, in case she changed her mind. Then, as soon as we were out of sight, I'd ease him to a stop in the woods. I'd stash the blanket and the saddle, the bridle and my stupid cowboy boots, and climb up on him bareback with the help of a tree stump.

My bare heels would give a little squeeze and Barr would pick up again, only this time with an easy plod, his head slung low, bobbing lazily in the sun while I stripped out of my shorts and top.

We settled into our pace, my clothes draped across his withers, my only rein a tuft of his mane wrapped loosely around my index finger. Barr led us wherever he wanted to go, through the woods and the upper pastures where we wouldn't see a soul. I trusted him. I rode in my underwear, my skinny legs dangling long over the ribs of his meaty belly, my ankles casting off the end of my lean shins into ballerina points. With each forward thrust of his muscled thigh, my butt bones rocked back and forth, a streak of oil and horsehair lathering a track down the inside of my leg. And with each rock, my torso shifted into itself more and more until I was in the delicious luxury of a full slump with my mouth hung open as wide as I needed it to be. No need to talk. No need even to think.

Sometimes Barr would stop altogether, standing in an empty field. He'd cock one back hoof up and shift his weight to rest. I'd lean over his neck, sliding my legs up and over his rump, until I was stretched out long across his back, as warm as sand, my arms draped around his neck, my head falling against the slab of his withers. We'd stay like that, for a long, quiet time, drifting in and out in the sun's warmth. And when Barr was ready to go, he'd shift his hoof back under him, hoisting us up a notch, and then take a baby step forward to rouse me.

I'd pull myself up, draping my legs back down over his ribs again, then lean over and give his neck a pat, pat. Barr would start up once more, carrying us along in his slow, easy plod, farther and farther away from Hideaway Farm.

THE SUMMER AFTER MY NOSE HEALED, Mom would line me up in the gravel driveway and snap Polaroids of me, hair held up in a bun on top of my head with one hand, our plywood-sided trailer as background. She'd pack me in a padded bra, tight Wrangler jeans, pink button-down with the collar flipped up, and sometimes a cowboy hat. She'd send these off to the Ford modeling agency in New York City, waiting for me to be discovered. And the ones she kept behind rode in her purse. She never knew when she might run into a nice older man who might like to have a look at me.

I have a stack of these pictures, the last remaining window of my youth to peer through. My sockets hold the pale gray eyes of a ghost, telling of a life in which I have little say. The rest of my face wears a look that says I eat men for breakfast, broken and smeared upon my morning toast.

AS SOON AS I'M SIXTEEN, Mom puts me on the pill so I won't get pregnant. I'm old enough now to date, and she has a few guys she'd like to see me go out with. The first is Debbie Miller's son. He saw me riding my horse and arranged it between Debbie and my mom. His name is Don. When I meet him, he reeks of Polo and sports a bushy black mustache. He is thirty-one.

My first date with Don is on his boat with Debbie as chaperon. Debbie lights up a cigarette and the platinum split ends of her frizzy perm flap along leathery tan shoulders with every thrust over the wake. Don cruises into the center of the lake and cuts the motor and we drift in the lazy sun beating down. Debbie has brought sandwiches, pink ham salad. She winks at Don when she hands him one. I think she is trying to tell him something, but I can't be sure. Sitting between mother and son, my stomach drains hollow. I'm famished but I can't seem to do more than nibble at the smooth spread from around the edges of the bun.

Debbie feigns a stretch and crawls off to the padded bench on the other side of the boat for a catnap, leaving me with Don on the little triangle deck in front. He reaches out to feather his fingertips along the strings of my bikini top. Don wants me to come to his condo, all on my own. He's got something he wants to show me. He tries to kiss my face, grating his thick skin against my own, as soft as a colt's underbelly. I scoot over a couple inches and talk fast about Dad's old cars. I want Debbie to wake up, to shout, "Don, in God's name what are you doing? Stop that!" I want her to make him feel bad, to stick a knife in his gut, to fillet him with guilt and shame. But she is giving her son his privacy and I stay where I am. They have been so nice to feed me lunch and to take me out for the day. I don't want to disappoint anybody. When Debbie wakes up, I jump into her arms with an enthusiasm that startles us both.

Don jerks the throttle and drives his boat fast, grating against white peaked waves, *Miami Vice* style, his jaw set against the fading sun and the protective bond I've suddenly forged with his mother. As we ease into the bay, I am so glad to see my own mother waiting in the parking lot that I leap onto the dock and run to her. She is leaning out the window of the car, waving wildly to Debbie and Don.

WE HAVE HIT THE END OF THE ROAD. The doctors can't find anything else wrong with me. I am on my heart medications with slight variations in dosage and frequency. But the big ticket, the big chance to get in there and *really* get to the bottom of it, is behind us.

At one time, we had a chance to do the open-heart and get some solid answers. But my doctor was too young and inexperienced to know how to handle my special case. Mom has spent her life trying to get competent medical care for her sick kid and it's all been in vain. I'm still sick and Dad lost his job last year on my birthday, so we don't even have the good medical coverage anymore.

We still occasionally go to church, and when we do, Mom tells everybody that I'll never get better and to please include me in their prayers. She'll be surprised if I live to twenty. The best we can hope for is to stabilize me with the meds I'm on. But my heart still races, I'm still out of breath, and I still walk around with my mouth hanging open. I still drink cans of chocolatey Ensure Plus and crunch on weight-gain wafers, only now knowing they don't do much of anything.

DAD NEEDS TO HAVE a heart-to-heart talk with me. In here: he motions to one of the empty bedrooms. He walks to the bed and I follow, apprehensive. He sits down on the edge and pats his knee for me to climb on like I was still a child. But I'm not. I'm sixteen. And I do not want to sit on my father. I teeter one sit bone on his knee and brace the rest of my weight on my other leg, which stretches as far away as possible.

Dad places a hand on my back. "I can't let you try out to be a lifeguard for the Y."

"But, Dad! It's the only thing I want to do for my first summer job. I can swim and I can—"

"Remember when you were little and people used to laugh at you out in public?"

I nod, hot tears welling up.

"Well, honey, I just can't see my little girl go out there in a bathing suit and get laughed at. You got no tits, no hips, no ass, Sissy. You look terrible in a bathing suit. Kids are cruel, sweetie, they'll just make fun of you. But don't worry about finding another job, Mom says she's gonna see if she can get you on at the hospital."

WITHOUT THE DOCTOR APPOINTMENTS, the extra hours of summer pile up, without boundaries or direction. The country holds no outer distractions to break up the time or keep your reality suspended in a busy world; no shopping malls to stroll through, no nearby restaurants, no Blockbuster Video. Time stretches out, and a single day can feel like four.

Most nights Dad tinkers alone in the garage. When he's with Mom, they scream at each other all the time. They fight about Dad losing his job. They fight about the money he lost. And they fight about the divorce they can't afford.

We're all stuck down on the farm together: restless, bored, anxious, stressed. Mom's shoes sit in the closet, ticking away. Me, Danny, and the foster kids stick to the plastic seats of the station wagon, sweltering, while she ducks in and out of stores to buy more: more clothes, more shoes, more concrete animals to line the hallway.

We have added on as many rooms as a former trailer could possibly spawn. We have six bedrooms, three baths, two living rooms, a freezer room, a laundry room, a den, a good dining room, three decks, and the back junk room where we, the children, and the wood spiders hide.

We have built a garage off the side of the log cabin, a pole barn to stack with hay, a junk barn for Dad's old parts to sit in, an extra bay to store the boat we bought out of the paper but never use. We have planted the slow-growing willows and fruit trees, graveled the drive so many times I have permanent calluses on my hands from fanning rocks, one shovelful at a time, from the dump-truck size pile we get every year.

The pool is up. The fence lines strung. The horses number ten. The tack room is stocked with every silver-conched saddle and matching show bridle, blanket, lead, and halter imaginable. Danny and I have won all the yellow, pink, and purple polyester ribbons that line the hutch shelves, and I have been runner-up Horse Queen in the Pickaway County Fair.

MY MOTHER IS STANDING next to the wood-burning stove, her arms crossed tightly before her, weight on one leg, her body stiff.

She says, "Well, what are you going to do about it, huh? You fairy-assed faggot, you goddamned fucking faggot?"

And as she is dripping out each word my father is getting more and more riled by her insults, seeing red. His anger at her boils, but it's his cowardice that runs like lava in the grooved pipeline to me. He charges, grabs my hair by the fistful.

"I'll show you what I'm going to do about it. No little fucking bitch of a slut is going to make me sick picking up her goddamned crusty Kleenexes." The coffee table is all that's between us. He is clutching the life out of the Kleenex, getting the germs all over him, his adrenaline-soaked palm mixing with its deadly hosts.

Mom has told him I drop them so he will have to pick them up; a premeditated attempt to sicken my father with clever trickery.

He takes the Kleenex, and as his voice gains momentum, my mother's trails off. Like a relay race in which she just puffed through the first leg, he is stepping in and now she can let go. My eyes are frozen wide, this can't be happening. I tell him that the Kleenex is Mr. Beck's; that he loses them when he's shuffling to the bathroom, that he can't help it because he's slow from the drugs.

My mother rolls her eyes: That's the most insane excuse she's ever heard spew out my mouth. He responds to her cue that I am lying, and he is prompted by the promise of the reward: Let her give him peace, please God, give him peace, just let him be, let him go back into his shell.

Oh, now I'm calling him a liar, I'm challenging his view. No little shit is going to call him a liar.

He takes my head down, down, smash my skull goes into the piercing corner of the coffee table. Pain splinters my face, my new nose, and ricochets, vibrating to all points over my scalp, like the crack of lightning that fingers its way through the sky, crack my face goes into the wood, the glass, the evil sharpness of this madness.

I cannot cry. I am going to die. There is no reason to cry when there is no hope you'll live. I am petrified wood, like Kawliga in the old song Mom and I used to sing in the car, stiff like my mother in the corner with her arms crossed. But then he pulls my head up, hair still clenched, with an urgency as if I'd been drowning in a metal tub of cold water while bobbing for apples and he, with an opportunity to save me, plucks my head from the water with great, shuddering force.

He is holding the Kleenex and I am crying now, No No No, as he is now teaching me the lesson I will take to my grave. Don't you ever leave another Kleenex around here again, and he is thrusting it to me because he wants to see me do it. He wants to see me place the Kleenex in my mouth and chew it up. And in that split second he knows I can't and that I'm testing his strength to make me, to see if he is man enough to not let his own daughter make a fool of him. I see it in his eyes, it is her voice that drives him, eggs him on and crack, dunk, again back into the corner and on the way down, which is a long way down because I am already five foot eight, I slice my eyes up in a plea to my mother for help.

"God, please," I scream, "help, Mom, he is going to kill me!"

And she is standing just where she was three minutes ago. Three minutes ago my life was different. Three minutes ago I could have made it out of here intact, but now...

And my mother, arms folded, body now relaxed and loose, is wearing the curly smile of a Cheshire cat, staring right at me, holding my eyes as I go down, crack, into the corner. I come up again to meet the growling promise that I will be killed by his fists or maybe he will just strangle me with his bare hands until I'm limp and he is huge, bellowing and at least two hundred and fifty pounds of angry Brahma bull and I have no reason to doubt now and I put the Kleenex into my mouth so slow, so dainty like it's a fluff of a ladyfinger from the Swiss Colony catalogue, hoping it doesn't touch anything as the paper sinks in to my saliva, the dried snot I

imagine as stale fibers of cotton candy; a rich, peppermint sugar puff from the bottom of Grandma Madge's
purse and it collapses into my tongue and begins its
meltdown, its digestion there in my mouth, and my father is screaming, eyes wild, his brows burrowing a deep
V down to his nose, rippling smaller ones over his forehead and he's still holding my hair, now at the back of
my head so I can't pull away, and I start chewing softly,
feeling cotton touch my fillings, cotton compress under
the weight of my molars, cotton go from dry to wet, dis-
solving into fine white bits that work their way up under
my gum and cheek. My father is threatening I had better
hurry up and fucking chew it up and swallow it because
I have two seconds before he kills me and—

"My God, Dan, you're not going to make her swallow it, are you? What kind of a no-good son of a bitch
would do that to their own daughter?"

And he stops because she has given him permission
to do so. He is off the hook from being a fucking faggot
and he can bear being a no-good son of a bitch because
he is a man that knows how to get respect from his children. They will listen to him, goddammit, or else he'll
kill them.

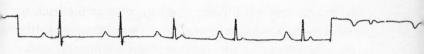

IT WAS THE SAME HOLLY HOBBIE CASE-worker who saved me—well, us—the summer of my junior year, when I was sixteen. And it was all by a fluke.

Since I couldn't be a lifeguard, Mom got me a job at the Lancaster Fairfield County Hospital as an assistant nurse aide. I walked the halls for a paycheck, the same halls I'd spent hours waiting in as a patient.

The program was run by the county and set up for high school kids. One of the requirements was to meet with a work counselor each week to make sure the stresses of working with hospital patients hadn't got our carefree childhood selves down.

Mom was still driving the foster kids into town for state-appointed therapy. She set it up so each child had a different counselor that she met with first, before they did. She tells the therapist that this one lies pathologically or that one has been violent, and reminds the kids on the way in that nobody will believe them if they try to act out to get removed.

On the way to counseling, Maria unfolds a piece of notebook paper and warbles out a song from the backseat; lines about how much she loves Mom but that maybe she should leave since she makes Mom so angry, but she'll still love her forever and she'll always be her Mommy. Mom lurches the car over to the gravel berm. She whips around in her seat and flails her fists while Maria tries to shield herself. "You listen here, you little slut, you ain't going nowhere. If you want out, the only place I'm taking you is back to your dad in his wheelchair and his fat beer buddies so he can pull your pants down again. You'd like that, wouldn't you?"

I BROKE DOWN when my work counselor asked me how it was going. Work was great, home was hell. I begged her not to tell. She said there was a law that could put her in jail if she didn't. She called up Holly Hobbie and everything unraveled.

HOLLY HOBBIE, WHOSE real name was Melissa, drove down to the house, drove into the dark tunnel that concealed us from the world, and pulled into the empty drive. Mom was at the back window with the gun in her pocket. The caseworker never came without calling first.

Melissa explained that her surprise visit was to talk to the kids about how they would feel about being adopted. Privately. It was the first time anyone had ever talked to any of us privately. *Private* was special. Private was scary. Either we were in trouble or they were. Either way, it was a big deal.

Melissa took the kids on a walk down the road and told them I was in town and had spilled it out. With some reassurance, Maria, Lloyd, and Ricky told her enough. When she walked back down the road with them, she beelined them straight into the back of her station wagon and went in to grab some clothes. That's the day Mom and Dad lost their license for foster care. And that's the day the caseworker first stumbled into the other wing where we kept Beck. We lost him, too.

Once back in Lancaster, Melissa found me in the hospital and told me that I could never tell them I did it, no matter how convincing and understanding Mom might seem. She gave me an emergency number for the agency and told me to call her at once if they found out. Melissa was scared for my life.

I FINISHED OUT THE REST OF MY DAY at the hospital, as if nothing had happened. But inside, I was glowing. I had a secret. I had single-handedly saved Maria, which was what I wanted to do all along—get her out—and I was able to save the rest of the kids to boot. I didn't know where they would go—float out into the sea of social service kids, playing the odds of finding a decent foster home—but still, they were out and that's all that mattered.

When I pulled in at the top of the road, I kept saying over and over, *Got to stay cool, got to not let my face show it, got to act normal, be upset and surprised*. Mom was waiting for me in the drive. "Did you do it? Now you can just tell me, we won't get mad. Did you do this to us," her voice works loose, "you no-good creeping motherfuckin'..."

My acting skills are polished. I feign shock, bewilderment. I cry with Mom at the kitchen table. She thinks out loud. "Do you think it was Annabelle when I bloodied Penny's nose on that trial ride? I wonder if Jim turned me in for kicking Lloyd in the stomach that time in the 4-H barn at the horse show." I am sickened. But my face shows nothing.

It only took four days for Mom to be smiling when I walked in.

Perched on the edge of the couch, she waved a tiny sliver of paper. "I found out who did it. Look at this."

It was a teeny tiny bit of paper with the emergency number I had microscopically encoded onto it, the one I had rolled into a pair of socks in the back of my underwear drawer. Mom had called the number and quietly placed the receiver down when Children's Services answered.

"Dan's on his way home right this second. You're dead meat, girl. He's going to kill you. You hear me? You're dead; you're not going to get through this one. They can lock me up for fucking ever but you are going to pay for what you did. You just wait." She's writhing with anticipation.

"Now, you get your ass out there and get some work done before your father gets home."

I STARTED CARRYING OUT paper bags of trash, out past the car in the gravel drive and over to the charred ash pile where I burned them by the road. When I came back in the house for the next load, I emptied the trash into the back of my closet, filled the bag with clothes, and stuffed a few pieces of paper on the top. Then at the last minute, crunching down the gravel drive, I flung each bag in the back of the station wagon. When I had enough clothes, I scooped up my little dog P. J., threw her in the front seat, and peeled out the drive, praying to

God I didn't meet Dad barreling down the road. I don't have the emergency number to the agency anymore. I have nowhere to go but to Debbie Miller's son. Mom's had me memorize his number so I know it by heart. Don will be there, waiting, waiting in his Polo-scented condo. He's thrilled I'm coming alone. He's got something he wants to show me. And I know I will have to let him. My mother has trained me well.

THE NEXT DAY, DAD TAKES MY CAR from the parking lot while I'm working. It has all my clothes in it and my little dog, too. I have nothing but the hospital uniform I'm wearing. I have to call Melissa.

She drives me to an emergency group home for teen runaways and delinquents. I've now become a foster kid. Melissa promised me a private home with a nice family but she couldn't find me one in time.

MOST FOSTER KIDS, by the time they reach my age, are hard and mean. They're pregnant. They steal. The concept of Mom and Dad went out with the tooth fairy and Santa. Once a teenage foster kid loops into the system, nobody takes a blow for them. They're beaten as the world watches, and no matter how many times they tell themselves they're a wanted kid, they know if they were, they wouldn't be here in the first place. It's simple logic.

Even if they regain some hope that this home's different, by the time the family sets down all their obsessive ground rules and punishments for a trial run with them, they know there are two sets of laws: one for the real kids, another for them. And foster parents are wary to take on a teen, no matter what the circumstances, because they know an overloaded underpaid caseworker will snake just about any lie down their throat to unload one off on them. Once you take a teen in, it's hard to get the caseworker to come out again and retrieve them. Like scratch-and-dent merchandise, foster kids come with a limited warranty. And Children's Services caseworkers act as time-share sales agents, hawking off sinking lakefront property and freshly painted lemons from the underbelly of America.

But I wasn't a jaded kid, just one whose life was in danger. Melissa tried to tell them I was different, that I wasn't a troublemaker, but the woman who ran the group home had heard it all before. I'd have to follow the curfew and personal checks just like the rest of the juveniles. Juveniles they called us. I was living with juveniles. Turn your parents in for child abuse, and you're set up with a bunch of delinquent misfits.

All during that summer, I was still working at the hospital. Melissa would drive down from Lancaster in the mornings, pick me up at the group home in Logan, then take me to work and drive me home. She insisted it was the least she could do for me. Sometimes I'd see her crying silently as she drove, the sun reflecting off her wet face. I think it may have had something to do with not believing Penny.

C'MON, SIS, PLEEEASE COME HOME. Please tell them you made it up and to drop the charges. C'mon, I miss you. Siiiiissssyyyy!"

Mom and Dad are waiting in the parking lot with the car running. They send Danny in about once a week to trot around the halls of the hospital to find me and beg me to come home. He's only ten.

"I miss you, too, Danny, but I can't. Melissa is counting on me to testify against Mom and Dad. She's counting on me, and if I came home now, they'd kill me."

"Mom said everything's forgiven, you're not in trouble anymore, Sis, she's not mad at you no more. If you just come home now and forget everything, she'll forgive you."

"Danny, I want to be with you but I just can't. I have to keep my job here and live in Logan, and Melissa would be really mad at me. I'm gonna see you soon. I promise."

Danny trudges out of the cafeteria and turns around at the double swing doors, squeezing his hands together in prayer and pleading for me to change my mind. I wipe my tears and put my head down on the lunch table. I hate to see him beg.

Every week Danny weaved his way through the hospital, looking for me, but I couldn't tell a soul. The last place I wanted my little brother to end up was in foster care.

BY THE TIME MY CASE got to the courtroom steps, I was less sure of anything than ever before. I could tell Melissa was getting tired of the extra time she had to spend on me. It was forty minutes each way between Logan and Lancaster and she had to fit it in before and after her regular work at the agency. And then there was the one and only counseling session she'd okayed for me to do. Mom had called Melissa and asked her if I'd do a

Don't

reconciliation session with them, to try and sort things out. I imagined Mom and Dad sitting in front of a therapist, begging me to come back home. I was prepared to be solemn and humble while their heads hung and they pleaded for my forgiveness.

Instead, Mom and Dad had found a counselor who wasn't part of Children's Services and didn't know anything about why I was in custody.

I sat sandwiched between them in the therapy room while Dad talked about how I'd stolen the family car and how they were worried sick, and Mom chimed in that she'd caught me climbing out the window to meet boys at the top of the road.

Our counselor was a big, lumbering black man, the same kind of black man Dad had pulled a gun on in the McDonald's drive-through not even a year ago when he approached our car window. But here Dad was saying "Yes, sir," and "No, sir," and telling him I was in a group home for juveniles and awaiting my court date on the unruly child charges they had filed against me. By the time it was my turn to talk, I'd already interrupted with "but" and "wait" a zillion times.

The therapist turned to me. "Did you take the car, Julie, and run away? Just answer the question, yes or no."

"Yeah, but I had—"

"Didn't you stop to think about how that might worry your mother and father? Did you not consider their feelings before you stole the family's car? And who did you run to that night? An older man? To spend the night, Julie?"

And it all went downhill from there.

That session, those records from that counseling

hour, traveled to court under Dad's armpit like a trump card, while Mom clutched to her chest a manila envelope with big markered letters pointing out for all to see, "Proof of Unruly Charges Against Julie Gregory."

It had just enough official bearing to unnerve me.

MY HEARING WAS AT EIGHT A.M. in the tiny downtown of Logan. Melissa wasn't there yet. I had walked the few blocks from the group home to the county courthouse. Dad sat, watching for me, on the wide winding staircase that led upstairs to the courtroom.

"Sissy, can you come outside with me? I really got to talk to you."

We sat on the courthouse steps in the summer morning sun. Dad took my hand in his and rested it on his knee. His eyes turned watery and he started to cry. He was crying for me, for what they were going to do to me when I got sent to detention, for how I'd get beaten with rubber hoses so the marks don't show.

Didn't I know why I was in court this morning? Was I a moron or what? It wasn't charges against them, it was charges against me for being unruly.

"Honey, they're only tricking you into coming to court so we can prosecute you for being out of control. Your mother and me have all the proof.

"Think about it, Sis, why do you think she put you in a group home? If you were a good kid, don't you think they'da put you with a regular family? And if she was on your side, why ain't she here now?"

I looked around. Melissa wasn't here. And it was almost time for the hearing. *But I had interviewed with a family. Melissa said it takes time; I wasn't in trouble, was I? I thought it was the agency that was taking them*

*to court for child abuse, not Mom and Dad filing
charges against me. Why isn't Melissa here? Maybe it is
a trick.*

"I'm telling you, Julie, the charges have already been
turned over to the court. If we had charges on us for being abusers, why aren't the other kids testifying? I'm
afraid for you, honey, if you try to come up with some
cockamamie child abuse shit on your own, I think
they're gonna see right through it. If they take you, Sis, I
won't be able to do a damn thing to get you out. They'll
keep you till you're twenty-one. I don't want to see this
happen to you, Julie."

My dad can beat me with his laced leather belt, with
his fists. He can kick his steel-toed boots in my stomach
till I feel like I'm going to die. He can brand me with
welts on my face, he can slam my head into the coffee
table corner, grab my hair and bolt my face against the
dashboard. But there was no way I could let some
stranger beat me, not with a rubber hose.

WHEN MELISSA ARRIVED, breathless, in the hallway,
Dad casually blocked her entrance to the courtroom. He
whispered in her ear and a slow red flush crept up over
her face. I could see her from where I sat inside the
courtroom, my heart racing. She tore away from Dad
when she spotted me.

"Julie, Dan just told me you're not going to testify,
that you're not going to tell the court anything. Honey,
we need you—I need you—to tell them about the abuse.
I need you to do the right thing!"

I sit slack on the hard bench. Hadn't I done the right
thing already? I saved the kids. How could I stand there
in front of strangers and tell them what Mom and Dad

did—with Mom and Dad and Danny sitting right there watching? How did I know the judge would believe me, especially after the black counselor? And Melissa didn't have anywhere else for me to go. There was no reward—no family—waiting for me after I did the right thing. There was only my own.

Melissa stared at me, waiting for my answer. I wanted to cry, I wanted her to reach out and pull me in to the safety of her long arms so I could just cry. *If you hold me, Melissa, if you put your arms around me, I'll do the right thing for you.*

But she didn't. And I didn't want to go back to a bunk bed in a lonely house with stupid old caretakers, doing it for the money. This way I'd at least get to be with Danny.

Since Melissa couldn't keep me in foster care without the court's backing and the court couldn't back her without proof or testimony of my abuse, they had no choice but to send me home.

I was relieved. It was probably me, I told myself, just having a rough time with adjusting to adolescence. Or, as Mom and the school counselor had decided in tenth grade, just an incredibly fertile imagination.

AND WHEN I RETURNED HOME, it was to a different family. Mom and Dad didn't fight. The guns stayed put. No bedroom doors creaked in the night. When Dad would suck in one of those deep sighs that always came before he exploded, Mom would "uh, uh" and reach out to slip her hand into his.

We had pot roast dinners and bedtime hugs. We watched TV together. Danny helped with the chores and Dad carried heavy things. It was the most blissful time

I'd ever known. We never talked about the terrible thing I did in ratting on Mom and Dad or how I'd made them have to claim bankruptcy by taking away their only income.

We just acted like a normal family. And I wasn't sick anymore. The whole time I was in foster care, I didn't take any heart medications because they all got left behind when I ran away. Instead of seeing doctors, I spent my free hours jumping off the diving board at the public pool and shopping for clothes with my hospital paychecks. It was going on six months since I'd seen a cardiologist, and Mom wasn't even buying me Ensure Plus anymore.

WHEN I WENT BACK TO SCHOOL that fall for senior year, just a few weeks after I returned home, I was so excited about my new life. I got an after-school job at Rax Roast Beef and would have my own money for school lunch, a discounted dinner at Rax, and, since I got to take the car to school on work days, I could stop off someplace and get breakfast. This was the year I was going to get good grades, this was the year I was going to have friends, this was the year I was going to be popular, I was thinking, maybe even do track or tennis.

I walk through the halls in my new clothes with my head up, clasping my new spiral notebooks against my chest, and a wake of whispers rises up behind me as I pass. I think they are signs of admiration. But as the day wears on, nobody speaks to me but my one friend Carmen, the only girl who'd taken me in after I was dumped. People I say hi to shoot me a sickly smile and walk quickly past. At my locker at the end of the day, Missy Morrison saunters up to me and asks point-blank, "Were you, like, in a foster home this summer?"

My face flushes and I look into my locker to hide a surge of tears. "No," I say, cool and casual. "Uhh! Where'd you hear that?"

"Well, it's like everybody knows."

Everybody did know. They all knew I was in a group home for bad kids. They all knew I'd been a green-haired freak in seventh grade. They all knew I made stuff up about Mom and lost my friends in eighth grade. And they all knew how stupid I was for failing algebra, French, and even the easiest class of all last year: Health.

ONE DAY IN LATE SEPTEMBER Mom asked me if I had a friend I could spend the night with. She was planning an overnight trail ride with Danny down at the Horseman's Camp and it happened to be on the same night that Dad was going out of town for a swap meet. They didn't want to leave me at home all alone and Mom thought I might like to spend the night with Carmen.

"You've grown up a lot, Sis, I think we can trust you now."

That delicious night of freedom, Carmen and I stayed up way past midnight. We jumped on her bed and collapsed into a massive pile of girly clothes we'd spent hours trying on. We ran barefoot across the warm pavement of the road during a thunderstorm, the steamy air smelling faintly of worm breath. We bought pizza subs from the Tarlton Tasty Freeze and fell asleep spooning each other in her bed, bursting out from under the covers with giggles, whispering, "Do you think

Martin Roberts from shop class is cute? Do you think Bruce Delorne likes me? Do you think Mr. Summers is gay?"

FOR SEVENTEEN YEARS, Mom had been fused to me. We had shared one long symbiotic breath. And when I did get out, Dad would drag me back like a rabid junkyard dog, tearing out of the garage after any boy from school that drove down our road to stop and say hello to me. In all those years of horse shows and trail rides, swimming in the pool, porch nights with Stink Pup and Ebony or snuggling with my P. J., I didn't have as much fun as the night I spent at Carmen's. And it wasn't just because I was away from home. It was because I now had Mom and Dad's permission and trust to stay out. It was because, deep down, I had a hunch they knew I did the right thing in God's eyes by turning them in. I had finally earned their respect. And I was thrilled.

THE NEXT MORNING, when I pulled from the wooded tunnel that encased our road, I saw before me a deserted smoldering football field of twisted metal, dusted with a thick layer of soot like a blackened catfish, where our six-bedroom double-wide mansion used to sprawl.

I took my foot off of the accelerator and let the wagon ease to a crawl. My brain was racing, "Oh. My. GOD. I left the curling iron on and burned the house down!"

I was going to be in soo much trouble. *OH MY GOD!* What if everybody was inside? Dead. Panic hit and I punched the gas, hauling the next hundred yards to the house. When I slammed into the gravel pit of our drive, Mom popped her head out of the log cabin.

"Oh, Mom, I'm so sorry, I'm so sorry." I ran out of the car. "Did I leave it on? Did I do it?"

"Did you do what, Julie?"

"The curling iron, Mom, did I leave the curling iron on and burn the house down?"

"Jesus, Julie, it was lightning. Your dad came home early this morning and it was just, gone, it'd already happened. There was nothing anybody could do about it."

Mom said that the fire inspector was already there by the time Dad came home; the neighbors had called the sheriff when they noticed billowy smoke roll over the treetops. The fire inspector cited our TV antenna as the culprit. It had been struck by lightning, which traveled down the wiring, and since we had a TV in every room, it caught all the walls on fire instantaneously, in one initial poof, causing an explosion that ignited the house in a torrent of roaring flames.

There is no way any of us, had we been in the house at the time, would have survived.

"We'd a never got out," Mom said. "Just praise God we're all okay."

I looked at the still-smoldering lot of blackened, warped aluminum. Adrenaline was coursing through me, the way it did after a twister drill at school. The danger was over, we all survived, and even though we lost our house, everything was going to be okay. And I was off the hook.

I began walking along the edges of the black cinder blocks the trailer was built on. One by one things I'd never see again flashed into my mind. My shoes, oh, those awesome light blue ones I loved so much, and then, my pink cashmere coat and . . . oh my God, where's P. J.? Where's P. J.? A sick panic turned my stomach.

I raced back up the walkway, shouting, "Mom! Where's P. J., where's my P. J., I can't find P. J.!"

"Julie." Mom faltered. "Look. She was in the house when it burned. Now just let it go. Dan tried to get her out last night but you know how she goes under the bed when it thunders."

"Dad tried to get her out last night? I thought he was at the swap meet."

"Jesus, I mean before he left the house, he tried to get her out of the house before he left, you know, to put her out in the pen. Now will you stop giving me a hard time?"

No, no, I can't take losing my P. J. You can take my coat and those shoes, the York remote control stereo with the detachable speakers, you can take my porcelain doll collection and all my books, even my baby pictures, but ohh, P. J., you must have been so scared, so alone. No, you just can't take my P. J., God, why? Why, God?

This is what I ask of God, to help me rise above and look down on below. To see how tragic this has been, how there was no reason that P. J. had to burn up like she did, how God must have had a greater plan in mind, and that I, as the small weak human I am, just can't see it yet. I say a prayer for my lost dog, for Mom and Dad, and to please, God, please let me see the ways that you have divinely woven for my life so I can understand why you did this to me. Please, God, show me the light.

DAD IS IN THE CAMPER, sitting on the top bunk in his cutoff jean shorts. He's got his head hung low and a few tears have squeaked out of his eyes, leaving skinny streaks in the dirt on his face. I climb up into the hallway of the camper and sit silently at his feet.

He lifts his head and I stand to hug him. He needs me, my dad. And I am strong. I can get our family through this. He sobs then, and this gives me permission to cry with him. He is talking in distant whispers: Why did it have to happen, how come it had to happen? When Dad is small, I am big and have all the answers.

"God had a greater plan in store for us, Dad, and now you and Mom can do the things you always wanted, now you guys can afford to get divorced." And that is what I believed from that point out. That fire was a god-send. P. J. was sacrificed so Mom and Dad could get the money they needed to be free from each other; free from the past and everything they did to each other. And if we needed to lose all our clothes, our photos, all our child-hood things, if this is what needed to happen, then God must have said it was to be so. I felt honored that I could see this loss in such a noble way. I clung to this thought tighter than my white Sunday school Bible, the edges of its pages sprayed luminous with gold leaf.

IT WAS A HUNDRED BUCKS. That was money my family could use, I could be a hero. I would be the one who saved us from starving until the insurance check came.

In the first days after the house burned down, Mom and Danny stayed with a man up the road she knew from trail rides, Dad hung out with his junkyard bud-dies in Columbus, and I got to stay wherever I could. We didn't really have a home base and it was easier just to split up. The next day I ran into some kids I knew from Lancaster, where I worked at Rax. By now everybody in the Tri-County area had heard my house burned down. But the advantage to being in Lancaster was that nobody there knew I'd been a foster kid. The boys were off for the drag races in Columbus, I was off work, and it all sounded like a good way to use up an otherwise empty day. I climbed into the back of their primered Firebird and they sped off down the highway.

We pulled into Columbus Motor Speedway and found the only patch of grass still available to park, a thin strip that ran along a makeshift stage where girls were lining up next to one another. *That's weird; so many girls all together at a racetrack.* I unfolded from out of the backseat and as my head shot up to my full height, I saw a sea of men bunched up around the front of the stage. And they saw me.

"Heyyyy, pretty lady, we can't wait to see youu—Yeeeehaaaa!"

It was a wet T-shirt contest and the announcer on the stage was spitting into the crackling mike. A hundred dollars was going to one of these six lucky ladies and it would be decided by the response from the men.

"And just in time—being driven right up to the stage—let's hear it, gentlemen, for our seventh pretty girlllll."

Pretty girl. No one ever called me that before. And the men erupted in hoots and hollers. I'd never heard anything like it. An entire population of men were hooting like bonobos at me.

I looked into the sea of faces. Some were wearing overalls. Others were just homely, their limp hair sticking out from under CAT ballcaps. Still others had whipped their hats off and were waving them in the air. They seemed to ache for me, leaning forward, hands pleading, as if to say: *Please join the other girls up there and give an old man a little joy in his life, will ya?*

It *was* money my family could use. Nobody knew I was here. The men wanted me to win. Maybe I did have a shot. Why not try to win the cash and turn it over to Dad? I envisioned me giving my parents a crisp hundred-dollar bill and Dad beaming with tears of joy. *All I do is let them pour water down my front.*

I stepped toward the stage. The men roared. I had only the same stuff on from the night before, and there I was, standing at the end of the lineup, blanking out the outside world, just like I'd done all those years in exam rooms. But this time, a ribbon of thought played over and over. *This hundred dollars is for Dad.* They touch the tip of the pitcher to my chest. *This hundred is going to bring us together in love.* They pour. The girl next to me peels off her top and the crowd goes wild. *As a family.* I do the same. *This hundred dollars is going to get Danny some school clothes so the kids don't make fun of him.* She takes her shorts off. *It's up to me to save my family. I can't be selfish.* And down my jeans slipped, until I stepped right out of them. The men surged below the rim of the stage, their blurry tattooed arms waving like tentacles. I gulped some air. I'd been holding my breath the whole time.

As cheering or boos weeded the girls out one by one, it came down to two of us, Miss Blond-banged long-hair, and me: innocent country girl. No makeup, plain-Jane clean, long, smooth colt legs that curved up to my thigh-high lacy purple Value City panties, my svelte look obtained from cans of food supplements and an inability to gain weight.

With a half-grin, Miss I've-definitely-done-this-before decided to up the ante and turned right around to show her bottom to the crowd, wiggle it for their frothy approval, bend all the way over and peel, ever so slowly, her own underwear down off her backside, like an elevator descending, right down past the backs of her knees, down over her calves, right down till they looped around her ankles like a silky rope.

The throng of guys just about whipped themselves into a pulsating frenzy and she jutted her head up, still hanging down around her ankles, to smile at me in a way that said, "Uh-huh. You're beat."

Guys were throwing off their hats, slapping each other, wiping their tears. I burst into my own genuine grin. My jig was up. I wanted the money so bad, *sooo* bad I could taste it, but I couldn't bring myself to do what she did. I leaned over and picked up my clothes, flipping them over me zigzag, and made my way daintily down the rickety stage steps.

LATER THAT DAY I saw my dad's junkyard buddy, Big Eddie. The second he spotted me, his face lit up. "Purple panties, purple panties." My eyes must have registered horror because he narrowed his to slits and said as mean as any Westside hood, "Don't believe me? Go find your dad. *He snapped the Polaroids.*"

DANNY AND I RAN AROUND with green-tinged sweaters coating our teeth and peed in the yard. We ate buckets of Halloween candy before bed, and in the mornings we took it to school stuffed in our pockets to take the place of cafeteria lunch. Butterfingers for breakfast, Snickers at noon, Smarties for snacks, and giant mixing bowls with a half-box of Lucky Charms and milk for dinner. We didn't even use the sugar bowl anymore. We just poured an inch-thick layer of white over our cereal straight from the five-pound bag.

Before Mom and Dad left, we all shacked up in a tiny pull-behind camper that a man up the road had loaned us. It was set up on cinderblocks and plunked out on the grass by the charred remains of the old homestead. The teeny dinette we squeezed around for dinner converted into a bed for Danny and me by dropping the table into the center hole and sticking the stained upholstered cushions on the plywood bench seats. Mom and Dad had the foam mattress on the bunk, separated from us only by the sink and two feet of countertop. We turned the five-gallon worm bucket into a toilet and set it out to the side of the garage because the camper didn't even have a commode.

And there we sat, waiting on the insurance money. Before we could get it, we had to try to remember every last thing that'd been stuffed into our six-bedroomed lair: Mom's hundreds of shoes, the back room piled almost to the ceiling with junk we'd bought but never used, our closets bulging with clothes, rooms cluttered with toys and furniture, heaped with Matchbox car collections and collectible china dolls.

We lined notebook pages full of items scribbled in

our child's writing, and sometimes we would be in school or in town and spot something else we'd owned but had forgotten all about. The memories of our lost belongings haunted me for years, triggered by something as small as a polka-dot top seen on a girl that I hadn't remembered I'd owned before the fire. We turned in our lists, along with the price and current value as best our young, predepreciation minds could muster, and were swept up in the enthusiasm over what new things we were going to get with the money.

Mom made endless lists of things to buy. Then organized her lists into further lists, trying to keep it all straight. We kept asking, "When's the check gonna come? When's the check gonna come?" But it kept inching closer and closer to cold, to November, to heavy skies, wet crimson leaves and daylight savings turning it dark by five o'clock. We had no money for anything, and Danny and I were still wearing the same clothes we had on the day the house burned down. Luckily for Danny, Mom had packed a small wardrobe for the two of them the night they went away. Me, I just had my original fire clothes and some polyester high-waters the Rax Roast Beef team gave me so I could still work a few days after school.

We knew the check had come the day we got off the school bus and there was a newly delivered washer and dryer sitting out by the well, still in their cardboard boxes because there was no house to hook them up in. Across the road two baby colts nuzzled from grain buckets, and a new four-horse trailer sat attached to a just-bought crew-cab truck, with dual wheels on the back. The next day, a gleaming white satellite dish loomed over our little camper. Mom doled out of her purse a hundred dollars each for me and Danny to spend at Value City. We felt rich.

Then she was gone.

Mom took off for Mexico with the man who loaned us the camper, the man from up the road—Barbwire Bob—a wiry high strung cowboy who used to be a horse showman. Dad stayed with us for a while, but by November, he had moved into a garage in Stoutsville and hung in its only window a big black POW-MIA flag that said, *"Kill 'em all, Let God sort 'em out."*

We couldn't go with Dad, because somebody had to stay and look after the horses, especially Mom's new colts that stood helpless in the tiny paddock across the road.

Dad took with him his own new crew-cab dually truck and the washer and dryer. The only thing that stayed behind with Danny and me and our five-gallon bucket and mixing bowls of cereal was the steady looming watch of a giant satellite dish. Too bad we didn't have a TV.

WE MADE IT THROUGH THOSE DAYS AND NIGHTS with the grace of two latchkey kids who were determined to keep our style and image intact—if only so the kids at school wouldn't know about us. We were on our own, and I was a mom for real now with Danny. Our isolated spot on the bus route made us the first ones on at six a.m. and the last ones off at night. We counted on the bus driver taking the same route every day, hoping that there would be no one to look out the windows as the bus turned around in our drive. We hid behind false confidence and presented ourselves to the world as first-class snobby-as-could-pull-off-in-present-circumstances kids. God, we hoped nobody called Children's Services.

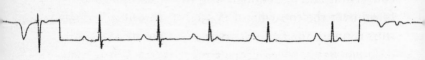

MOM AND BARBWIRE BOB CAME BACK before Christmas and moved a used single-wide trailer over the black scorched earth where our double-wide used to sit. I worked two jobs, went to school, and stayed away as much as possible. Nobody came to my high school graduation; not Mom, not Dad, not Danny. Two months later, Mom loaded me up in the station wagon and dropped me off in the Kroger's parking lot.

All that summer, she'd been talking on the phone to an older man who wanted to marry me. An older man in the Army, with a harelip and a white Firebird, complete with a hood-size sticker of that great winged bird on the front of the car. And now he was calling every week, talking to Mom about how he could get me till death do us part.

"Julie, look, do you think anybody is going to want to marry a sick thing like you? This man is in the *Army,* he's got a good *job,* let him take care of you!"

Mom reasoned that if she set me loose in a parking

lot with just a paper bag full of clothes to my name, I would be so scared that I'd call him to come get me.

But as soon as she drove off, I ran like hell. I hitch-hiked to Columbus and got a job out of the paper with an environmental canvassing group. I bought an old convertible and just enough stuff to load it up and flop a futon over the top when I needed to run. And I didn't stop running for three years; ten moves through three different states, never a forwarding address or my name on a lease. Once, I made the mistake of giving Mom my address, only to get a box in the mail full of cheap stuffed animals and gold-plated ankle bracelets from the same guy that was still calling her about me.

Most times I lived just one state away, and some summer weekends, when I was missing my brother and feeling lost without a family, I'd cruise down to Lancaster's Value City and other old stomping grounds. And sometimes I'd drive down into the holler of the country, down into the tangle of treetops, pull into the gravel drive, and step out into the outdoor concert of bird song, dragonflies, and locust calls. Danny would bound out to the drive like a puppy and fling his arms around me, just like he used to with Dad.

I have a picture of Danny when he's twelve, still living with Mom. He's driving my old Buick convertible with the top down, barreling down our dirt road, high spindly fields of green whizzing by. I've climbed out the window and spread myself across the hood of the car, hooking one arm around the antenna and an ankle around the hood emblem and snapped the photo: his head is tossed back in the sun as he speeds down the road, laughing over our momentary joy, a drop of laughter in our bucket full of pain.

Each time I'd come down, Barbwire Bob had built on a new deck or tacked up a new pressboard addition. And Mom had started collecting concrete animals, clothes, and shoes all over again.

There were afternoons when it was just Mom and me, when Danny was still in school and we went off and did things together; rode the horses, got in the pool, stroked the fluorescent green tree frogs that still suctioned themselves under the blue plastic pool liner. We never talked about the past or how I'd outrun my medical condition. And after our day, we'd sit at the kitchen table and she'd tell me what a no-good son of a bitch my father was, while I sat nodding I know, Mom, I know.

MOM AND I SIT IN THE LITTLE TRUCK. We're at the Volunteers of America thrift store in Lancaster, the rain has started to rail against the windows, and Mom has me trapped, talking venom about Dad. I know the score. "Uh-huh," I say, "I know."

Today she is specifically ranting about what an asinine bastard he is and how he borrowed from her share of the insurance money and was supposed to pay her back with interest, but now he's saying he doesn't have to, that they're even-steven.

I take this opportunity to once again remind her of God's will for us, how he miraculously and divinely caused lightning to hit that night, of all nights—the only one we were all away—and burn the house down, so that the two of them could afford to get divorced.

"I think that was pretty good timing on," I turn my palms up to heaven, "His part."

My mother shifts to look at me like I am the stupidest thing she's ever seen. She drops her jaw and rolls her eyes. "Oh, cooome'mon, what are you, some kind of moron? You think *God* burned that house down? It was your father. *He's an electrician, Julie.*" She slaps her knee. "My God." She looks out the window and humphs. "You are such an idiot. You think we all just *happened* to be 'away'? How do you think I have a stack of pictures that were in the log cabin? They just open the door and walk in there? Huhhh?" She is seething, that little blob of white spit sitting smack in the middle of her bottom lip.

My eyes lock straight ahead on the rain racing down the windshield, my mind reeling. *That's why she was in the log cabin that day; she was looking through the things he stashed in there. That's how come she still has Danny's and my birth certificates. That's how come they had a cache of clothes to last them.* It slowly comes together as if she's just raised the shade on a window I never knew existed.

"But . . ." my brain hurts, "but what about P. J.?"

"Oh, your asshole father just left her there." I cannot comprehend. How could anyone lock a little soft, curly-haired Shih Tzu in a house, then torch it? How could anyone breed a dog and sell off her puppies for years and years and pay her back by burning her alive? Tears stream down my face, matching the windshield.

"Oh, Jesus, that dog pissed my house full. I hated that dog. He just left her inside. That's what kind of a sick son of a bitch he is, you see?"

I glance over to her and catch sight of that little white drop bobbing on her lip, that speck I have watched in silence my whole life. A slow rage boils in me. God, I want to reach out and smear it off of her, I want to claw my fingers into the insides of her cheek and tear the flesh from her rancid mouth.

I sit there, caught. All this time, I thought it was God that delivered us from hell when it was my fucking dad who used his electrical rat-trapping to wire our house up to burn it to a crisp. And it was the two of them who arranged it so we'd all be away. And they did it after I came back from foster care, after they'd filed bankruptcy—that's why we were such a kind family for those three weeks; their plan was in place. And it was the two of them who split the insurance money. And all her kids got was a hundred fucking dollars each to replace all their belongings. And we were so naïve, we felt humbled by her generosity. And Danny and I used a bucket for a toilet while she traipsed through Mexico with Barbwire Bob. And Dad had a satellite dish installed and a washer and dryer delivered right to the little swing door of the pull-behind camper when his own kids didn't even have a pot to piss in.

At that moment, I lost my faith in God. My belief in God's will, the only thing that allowed me to find the meaning in the meaningless, was shattered, erased, stripped from my heart, and done so in a way that told me I was stupid for even thinking it existed in the first place.

I'm tired. My lids are so heavy. I could just lean against the truck and sleep.

My soft voice, barely audible, chokes. "We should go in before the store closes."

Mom said, "Jesus, Julie, I thought you knew. It was so obvious."

"No, I didn't know."

And I was still crying. I was crying for P. J., I was crying for everything fucked up in the world that nobody could do a goddamned thing about.

THE YEAR I TURNED TWENTY-ONE, I moved back to Ohio. I hadn't planned it, I just lost the juice to keep driving. It was one of my weekend trips down to the country and Mom had since given me a key, so I could come down anytime, whether she was home or not. I pulled in one afternoon when no one was home and riffled through her dresser, looking for some cutoffs to wear around the house. There in the bottom drawer, under stacks of pastel shorts, was a bulky manila envelope that read "Proof of Unruly Charges Against Julie Gregory."

I sank over the edge of the waterbed and ripped it open. Out spilled a pile of folded-up notes, handwritten on lined paper, torn from spiral notebooks, the same kind of notes I used to pass to my friends in class.

A couple of the letters were real ones from Missy and Carmen, but the others were nothing like our girly notes from seventh grade. Racing over the lines, I read of plots to run away and plans to be picked up at the top of the road by older men. I read lines that slurred, "Fuck my mother, that no-good bitch . . ." and "I'll do it for 50 bucks . . ." then digressing into profanity that flamed my face with blush. The words were written in big loopy letters to match my own and signed with my name. There were even answers signed by my friends. I stared at the letters, knowing they weren't mine, and there, scarcely visible to the untrained eye, was the unmistakable trace of Mom's shaky cursive writing.

After that, I didn't have the energy to drive any farther than Columbus. I opened the Sunday paper, and took the first cheap apartment I found. I didn't have the heart to run anymore. In fact, it was my heart that was sick, but I didn't know why. The symptoms of my childhood were starting to come back and I was beginning to think I might even die before I hit twenty-five.

And after all these years, I still float through the day with rumbling hunger pains and collapse into bed at night, starving. The skinny and ravenous hospital girl of thirteen, the girl whose mother would not feed her, has given way to the skinny and ravenous girl of twenty-three, who cannot feed herself. The girl whose life was held upright with stiffly knitted illusions is now the girl starting to unravel.

I wake in the morning and mix up a box of chocolate cake batter. I eat the whole bowl with a tablespoon and spend the rest of the day asleep or aching, my muscles like strands of flakey pot roast, falling off my bones.

My scalp is burning, searing. There are two cave-ins on each side of my head above my ears in the pockets of my scalp, indents from the vise that is collapsing my skull. The pockets slowly pool with lead liquid. I push in on them to relieve the pressure and a wave of nausea boils over me. It feels like the corner of the coffee table is still in there. My breath comes in shallow dips, my heart races upon rising, sometimes I black out on the toilet. I wake up on the floor, shaped around the tub like a chalk-drawn body at a crime scene. There has got to be something wrong with me.

I trek back down to good old Dr. Strong in Lancaster, the doctor who took my case after my heart cath. He half-heartedly listens to my heart and tosses me some advice on what might be wrong with me now.

He doesn't ask me if I am eating. I don't know that I'm not. The way I care for myself is no different than the way Mom taught me to, following the doctor's advice.

But Dr. Strong has lost interest in the pursuit of my heart condition and my mother has passed the baton to me. I am the only one running with it now.

AND I AM STILL ONLY a phone call away from my mother.

We go shopping and she lopes down an aisle toward me and the cart, clutching a stuffed animal, singsonging, "Will you buy it for me, Sissy? Huh, huh? Pleeaase." She stands at the checkout with her fingers looped through the slots of the metal cart, sneaking things off the candy rack onto the conveyer belt, while I unload the basket and pay for everything. I am the mother of my mother and as I age, she regresses.

And this is when I swing wildly from identity to identity, either elevating to be Mom's therapist or regressing to the stupid child she trumps, whatever it is my mother needs.

About every other month, I get a call from Danny to come take the gun out of Mom's mouth or the bottle of pills from her grip. It's over with her and Bob, and when she tried to go back to Dad, she found out about his girl-friend. This time she's locked herself in his truck and is going to do it. For real. Danny doesn't know how many pills, if any, she swallowed. I race the forty miles down to Dad's garage. My little brother has mouthed to her through the tinted window that I'm on my way.

Now I am the therapist. I sit on the stained cloth seat of the truck, bunched right up against her back, spooning her, and wrestle the bottle from her fingers clawing around it.

She's sobbing. "If that no-good, faggot-assed, wife-beating, paranoid-crazy, cocksucking son of a bitch don't want me, who will? Who's gonna take me?"

I try to explain that if Dad is all these things, if he causes so much pain, then why does she want him to want her? "Because if I can't make him want me," she wails, "who will?"

I have traded her for the pills she clutches a colorful publication called *Sweetheart Magazine*. I read about it in *People* and sent away for a copy to have on hand for her next suicide attempt. It's a personals magazine that lists all the lonely ranchers and mountain men that dot the remote plains of Montana, complete with half-page intimate write-ups and full-color portraits. I dangle it in front of her and flip through the pages, ooing and ah-hing over lonesome cowboys with wide Chiclet teeth and big Western hats and pointing at bold-type ads that order up: "Wife Wanted." Her eyes take the bait, and as I soften her fingers from around the bottle, I slip the magazine in unnoticed. This is the thing to sate her: the promise of a man to latch on to, from one monkey bar to the next, and to trade in her death for the hope of a life with another.

But then I am the child. And it is Danny and I, down on the farm, and she is the raging mother who has always frightened us, kept us in a state of held breath. She degrades us with sharp logic and we cannot defy the truth of her words: We *are* dumb kids; we did get bad grades, we do look sickly. She will press her fingers to weak bruised joints to make us fold.

She stands before a mirror and demands that I take pictures of her, while she barks at Danny to pivot the mirror just so, so that the picture I take is an exact replica of the reflection she's put in the glass. These are the pictures she sends to the men in the magazine. Her new hopes have restored her supremacy.

While I am waiting for Danny to reposition the mirror for the next shot, I am lost in thought, thinking about how Mom places all of us as mirrors around her, demanding we reflect back exactly what she needs to see, at precisely the right angle. And if we don't, she strikes out to break the glass.

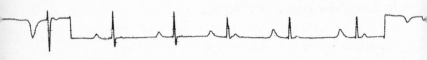

A T AGE TWENTY-FOUR I AM GOING back to school.

I was walking the aisles of a used-book store when I picked up a child's encyclopedia. The primary colors and simple text were so exciting that I plunked down right there on the floor with it, devouring the basic fourth-grade curriculum I'd missed along the way. And after that, I was hungry enough to try to learn what I was too sick to grasp as a kid. Since I don't have an actual high school diploma——thanks to losing that senior year mythology book I didn't have the dough to replace—I lie on the application for community college and somehow fool them into accepting me.

With just enough food coursing through me to make it out of the house three times a week to class, I muster up the energy to go. I want to find out if I'm crazy like Mom and Dad said, if I am stupid like high school confirmed. I want to know if I have brain damage like Mom's always told me. Going to school, especially in Columbus, is the only way I can find out in private, to hide the shame that I am all those things.

I take meticulous notes, study the solar system, Copernicus and Tycho Brahe. I read *The Name of the Rose* and great works of literature and learn that the Upanishads have the same creation stories that the Bible claims as its own. My mind is expanding and my grades are easy A's and B's. I cannot get enough of the possibility I might be even a little bit smart.

But my sickness is sneaking back. A few months into my second year, I can't keep up, just like I couldn't keep up on the farm. My heart races whenever I stand. I tremble as I mix a box of cake batter for breakfast. I study in bed, fudge papers, and keep missing class because I can't get out the door. I tell my instructors I'm going to have to withdraw for a while because I have a mysterious heart condition, left over from childhood. Because, for God's sake, what else could be wrong with me?

I MEET RAY: brilliant blue eyes, lean physique, a mop of unruly hair. Ray's a local musician who dresses like Frank Sinatra and blows hard-core punk out the end of his saxophone. I mix him up and pour him into an IV bag that I then inject into my arm. We are inseparable. Every day, I get nothing done. I eat my cake batter and live for Ray. His touch, his ways, anything he wants to inflict upon me. Neck bruises, teeth marks, late-night calls to come get him because the fifth of vodka he drank has him clinging to a wall on High Street. I question none of it and somehow, it is the happiest time of my sickened life.

BUT THINGS ARE CRASHING. Ray is moving to San Francisco at the end of the month and I can't function without him.

He snorts cat tranquilizer and crawls in my door, scoots across the floor, and oozes into bed. I live drug-free with only my devil's food cake batter to sedate me. We talk about things he doesn't remember the next morning; plans for me coming with him, plans for us staying together. He is slipping from me and I can't claw any harder to get inside him. We stop eating, stop speaking. Our choppy, punctuated words stab each other and we can't get them flowing again. I don't care about his drugs, his alcohol, his inability to match socks before he puts them on. I only know that, just as it was with my mother, I'll die without him.

Quaking apart, we understand each other only on a sexual plane. I mark little stars on my calendar for each day, each time we are together, as the only tangible proof I have that yes, he still wants me. I study my calendar squares with their tiny stars for clues to reality; some days there are many, other days are sparse. Several starred days in a row make a visual pattern that can be extrapolated into the future. The future when everything is better; the future when it's all different. The future I've been living in hope of my whole life.

When Ray stays away, I take the calendar to bed with me and nestle my tear-moist face to the squares with the most stars, willing more days like these. I wake in the morning with them stained in a trail down my cheekbone, like Cracker Jack tattoos. I contentedly wear the stars of Ray through the day, and break into quiet hysterics when I catch my face in the mirror and see they are fading.

In the final days, Ray takes what he wants when he wants and I have nothing but an insatiable urgency and passive comfort in signing my body over to him for as long as he'll have me.

I HAVE SIGNED UP FOR SUMMER QUARTER—a light load of two classes—determined not to be completely engulfed by Ray. I slip into abnormal psych class a half hour late one sticky July afternoon. I am there with greasy hair and sweaters on my teeth and a few anemic-looking bruises deep and purple on my bare legs. I slump in the back row, doodling as my slow country comrades hold up the class talking about their twice-removed cousin Ernie who they think had the mental disorder we just discussed. Didn't they ever read that new psychology students always identify with at least some of the disorders and start diagnosing themselves and their families? Don't they realize they're doing that? God, I hate students. My head swaddles down into the protective nest of my arms, curled on the desk.

The professor's soft voice moves on to a specific kind of child abuse:

> The perpetrator, usually a mother, makes an otherwise healthy child sick in order to seek continued medical care.

Mother...Make...Sick.

> The mothers who do this commonly have a history of traumatic abuse or neglect suffered in their early life.

I lift my head from my arms. A line of drool pools from my bottom lip down to the desk.

> Since the trauma or neglect was inflicted by her primary caretakers, the perpetrator gets a latent

parental need fulfilled from interacting with doctors, who are universally recognized caretakers and authority figures.

I sit up.

The doctor rarely finds anything actually wrong with the child, but the mother goes from doctor to doctor, pursuing tests and surgeries. Sometimes the mother fabricates the symptoms, sometimes she causes them. Sometimes the child is maimed, sometimes the child becomes sick from a combination of drugs and surgeries. Sometimes the child dies.

This form of child abuse is called Munchausen by proxy, or MBP.

I TRY TO SHAKE THE HAZE from my head. Shards of glass swarm in from all sides. The sound is deafening as they rush and fuse together. Then silence. The cracked mirror I'm staring in reflects back a sick, lost face, bottom lip gaped open, breath strained.

I jettison my chair and run out of the room. My legs buckle in the hallway and I drag myself into the brick stairwell.

My body, sliced, diced, and probed away from me for nothing.

I dig my fingers into the bricks and pull myself up until I'm leaning against the wall and quietly hitting my head.

They just did the tests, never questioned any of it.

I have all the missing parts to the real truth.

It was her all along.

The pieces are flying through me, trying to slide into their rightful places so I can put it together. I do not want to know.

It was my sacrifice to keep her alive.

I do not want to know.

So I could stay alive.

I do not want to.

Slam.

Know.

If she died, I died.

I do not want to.

CRACK.

Know.

I MAKE AN EMERGENCY APPOINTMENT to see Myrna at the Family Center. She's been my sliding-scale therapist for the last two months while I try to untangle from Ray. I pull the five-dollar fee from my stash, get in the car, and numbly drive to her. I sit in the waiting room, totally blank. I am waiting to come undone. I am barely holding my edges together, keeping myself from slipping away even further.

I sit on her couch and topple onto my side, panting, hysterical. I manage to get out what happened in class, what I learned happened to me. How it must be true because everything happened, everything happened: my mother, my heart catheterization, nobody finding anything wrong, my emergency room poisonings with Grandma Madge, my nose operation with my face in a cast, the tube they shoved in my urethra, and *oh, my God, oh, my God,* I am just now factoring in what I blurted out to the nurse when I was thirteen and how they sedated the truth away.

Myrna sits calmly, trying to make out the broken details that she's never heard before because we never got past Ray. I think she thinks I'm crazy. She has no comfort to offer, just coolness and detachment. She noisily uncrinkles another cough drop and pops it in her mouth.

Then she folds her fingers over her knee.

"(Suck) You know, Julie, when some of my clients are upset (sluurrp), I suggest they go home and take a nice looonng bath to relax. Have you ever tried to take a warm bath or perhaps to even (crunch) *journal*?"

You could wake up a Kafka roach and Myrna would still be sucking on her cough drops and telling you to go home and take a bath.

I SPEND THE NEXT TWO DAYS pacing my apartment, pacing the streets in the rain at four A.M., popping Sominex and trying to sleep, even if just for twenty minutes. I go to the grocery store, but my mind has me back in the hospital. People are crowding me, touching me, fingering out for me.

I shrink my shoulders together and walk as thinly as I can. I keep my legs and limbs close to my body. I cannot risk a wrist or an ankle being caught as I walk past. They are watching me shuffle down the aisles of frozen foods, they peer out from behind walls of cocktail onions and baby gherkins. They eyeball me at the checkout line, hold me at bay with their carts, looking me up and down. I can hear their thoughts. They are deciding whether I, with my sickliness and inability to sustain a healthy interest in sports, am worthy of even being alive.

Ray is gone and I don't remember a thing from my

psych class one week ago. I link my agitated state to getting a shutoff notice for the electricity in the mail. My hospital flashbacks fall through the cracks into my buried unconscious.

When I collapse onto the floor of my little apartment two nights later, my hands fly before me and curl into crow's feet. The faster I breathe, the more they kink. They curl and curl until they are frozen and knotty, deformed and clawing, right before my face.

I WAKE UP IN A FREE SHELTER for battered and mentally ill women. When I am coherent enough to talk, I try to tell them what happened, how I wasn't sick, how she made it all up. My stout corn-fed nurse goes pat, pat, "Oh, now, that's all right, honey. You don't try to talk."

My little brother Danny is the person they call. Sitting on my bed, he cries at the sight of me. I try to talk to him, to get a witness, so I know I'm not crazy.

"Danny, do you remember Mom taking you to get asthma treatments?"

Danny shakes his head no.

"Don't you remember the guns? Danny, you put one up to Dad's head that time after the house burned down, when we were all cooped up in the little pull-behind camper?"

"I don't remember, Sis."

"What about when I was in the hospital for my heart, getting that surgery?"

Danny wipes his eyes and his forehead constricts into thick folds of bottled-up emotion, just like my father's. He squeezes his eyes tight and tries to steady his quivering lip. "Sis," his voice cracks, "I can't really remember anything from when I was little." His fists are balled up and stuck on his thighs. "Nothing from before I was about fifteen."

And that's how old Danny was when he finally got away from Mom and went to live with Dad.

THE INDIAN PSYCHOLOGIST assigned to me thought I was nuts, too.

"Okay. Now vat is this thing you calling mooonch-hazen prozy? I never heard of that." She eyes me suspiciously from under her bushy brows, looking to catch a glint of my particular delusion so she can prescribe the right psychotropic.

"Can you explain to me one more time?"

I CHECKED MYSELF OUT OF THE SHELTER four days later and moved into a house of mirrors.

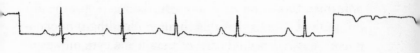

MY HOUSE OF MIRRORS is a ramshackle farmhouse that sits just a mile from the hospital where I was operated on. The rent is next to nothing. There's no heat upstairs. Even though I live in the city, the house is isolated, surrounded by woods, sitting on the dead end of a street, its foundation sinking slowly into the dense ravine below.

I stand in the largest room of the house, the walls hung with frameless mirrors salvaged from a dance studio. No furniture. Wood floors. Just me and the mirrors. This is where I live now. There is no one who can help me.

I look in the largest mirror. She's a natural beauty. I'm a sickened beauty. I'm beautiful, but with an inch-thick layer of sick covering me. It's in the dark slashes under my eyes, it's in the dull skin of my face, the flakes peeling from my lips, the cloudy glaze over my pupils, my heavy labored breath, the dampened feel that clings to me.

I could get rid of that layer, I could purge it out and polish myself to beautiful, if I could just stop making myself sick. But I can't stop. I can't stop. It's in my cells.

It's in my blood. It's in my survival instinct that was switched at birth. I've been hardwired for death, or if not death direct, then the absence of a thrust toward health.

Just to cover the basics, I take a part-time job as a receptionist, stuffing my long body under the cramped appointment desk of a natural medical clinic. I got the job thinking I could get discounted health services—nutritional counseling, detox treatments, vitamin supplements. Instead I work full days making continuous appointments for a steady stream of regular clients who seem to delight in having something wrong with them. One woman excitedly pulls a jar out of her purse with a long roundworm coiled in the bottom of it, showing everyone what the clinic has done for her. The worst part is making appointments for the mothers who stand at the desk and talk to anyone who'll listen about all the symptoms their kid has. I look behind the mother, straight into the faint eyes of the child, and I think we must be like the foster kids, able to talk without words.

"Sorry," I lie, "we don't have a free appointment for—well—it looks like several weeks." I schedule them on a day I'm off and sometimes forget to write their names in the appointment book, knowing the medical center will be too swamped to see them if they're not in a scheduled slot.

As long as I'm between home and the clinic I do all right. But out in the real world, I feel like prey. I slink around and can feel people looking at me. I feel their eyes boring into me. I feel what they're thinking: *Watch her, she could go off anytime.*

But within the walls of my farmhouse, I climb out of

the protective shell, my arms slowly rise like a phoenix, and I dance, wail, fly around the room and then collapse, crying, in front of my mirrors. In the winter light that streams through the large windows, I start to see in the mirror what it is I really look like, instead of what I was trained from the womb to see. I do not write about it. I do not talk about it. I do not know what I am doing. But just like a baby bird, I am blinking once-sealed eyes and unfolding damp wings. I cannot articulate the past. A part of me knows it's there, lurking, just behind what I can acknowledge, but it is not within sight. And I am keeping it that way.

I STILL TALK TO MY MOTHER, because I need to. I am a half-formed larva without her. She lives in Montana now, on the reservation, in a trailer with her American Indian lover. I speak to her as if nothing has happened, as if everything is fine. I still try to extract love from her. I still take her suicide calls in the middle of the night and try to talk her out of the gun or the overdose from two thousand miles away. I am the only one who can save her. I could not live with myself if my mother died because I refused to do what she trained me so well for.

Some weeks she calls me soft, ready to open. She says, "Sis, it ties me up in knots, I feel like you got a lot to get out—about the past..." *I start to weep, I've got to tell her I know what she did.* "...You're never going to justify what happened in the past..." *And why. And then I need to hear her cry for me...* "I don't understand it." *The words are dammed at the top of my throat, where they've always been since I sat on the examining room table, clucking my protests to Mom's made-up symptoms. The words dam at the top of my throat, with twenty years of river raging behind them, roaring, ready to push, rush, out into her, along with a torrent of tears.* "I don't know why he does the things he does. I just forgave him." *I swallow.* "A person tries. I tried. To keep the marriage together, to give you kids a good life." *The moment is gone.* "Here I am, in my fifties, trying to make ends meet. You know when I was back there last, they didn't buy me one meal, not one meal when I was out there. I mean it cost me a lot, I got two kids in college, but you know I'll do that, take it all on myself."

Her threads to reality are frayed bare. And her two kids in college are funded by their own sweat and blood.

SPRING THAWS THE FARMHOUSE, and in front of the mirrors, my breasts begin to form. They get white, tigerlike stretch marks on their sides from a burst of growth. My hipbones expand like a time-lapse flower in bloom. I grow like a girl in puberty. The pod I was stuffed into has perforated breaks in the skin, and I, ever so painfully, am unlacing myself from its tight shell. I use my fingertips to tug and pull the laces loose, unfurling myself from the cocoon I've been kept in, folding and falling, jutting the angles of crooked, atrophied limbs out of its hold.

I touch my face in the mirror, study it for hours. I need to see what my face says. What my expressions look like to others, what my eyes do, whether my face twitches, like hers.

Away from the mirror, I do not register that I am pretty. I cannot comprehend I have an attractive body. Or that it holds in its untapped wisdom the potential to heal itself. My instincts are wound tightly into a ball of fishing line, so tangled and knotted that it will take months of daily, delicate picking to see loops in the line and pull them free.

I curl my body up in front of the mirror; skin and bones, the ribs in my back casting curved shadows over my thin skin. I study my tiny, blue veins, fascinated by the light pulse that pushes blood through on its own; an affirmation that I am living. I do not have to pump the blood myself; it is my heart that keeps me alive.

I look at every part of myself through the mirror, wanting to see what anyone outside my skin would see. My hands, they look so beautiful, I turn them around and around in the mirror, mesmerized. I look at my face again, soft and childlike, my body, lean and lithe. I step away from the mirror but nothing comes with me. The moment I lose contact with my reflection, I lose touch with what I see there.

My mind is imprinted with the image of a sickly reverberation of what I felt like inside and believed to be true of myself for all of my twenty-six years: that I am some bizarre, frail creature, destined to die early. My mind's eye sees me as stooped and wasted, with dark greasy hair, a slaughterhouse horse's long, sunken face, drooping bottom lip, absent eyes. Since that is what I believe, that is how I feel. Since that is how I feel, that is how I act. And since that is how I act, that is how the world treats me.

So I step back in the mirror and there she is again, that girl, that strange girl that everyone else sees. I reach my fingers out to feel her face. My eyes cannot get over it. They peer at her suspiciously. Surely this is not me staring back? Truth in my mind and truth in the mirror are complete opposites. And I am split down the middle, straddling the chasm between two worlds, flitting back and forth between the world I know and the one that exists in the glass. It will take three years of pacing between the two before I can finally bring them together.

LIFE IN THIS RAW, NEW STATE is slow and infantile. My developmental levels are stunted; I take the baby steps of a toddler when I live as a walking, talking woman.

And I still can't eat.

When I look in the fridge, I see groceries, but I don't see food. My stomach growls; but there is no appetite.

Appetite and hunger are different. Appetite is the mental prompting that kicks the auto-response into drive so you actually reach out, take the food, put it in your mouth, chew, and swallow. I learned this in my first psychology course. Eating isn't just a physical need; it starts in the mind, generating hunger, which then should trigger the body to ingest food. I have no sparks between these plugs.

Unless I'm touched. Touch me and I'll eat anything for you. Stroke my back, hold me like a baby, grab and maul my body, and I turn ravenous.

I remember from class that when babies are touched, the hypothalamus in their brain is activated and sends out a message to feed. When babies aren't touched, the hypothalamus does not send the signal to eat and they starve. Would it be any different for an adult who was stunted developmentally? If a person is frozen at the level of an infant, why would it be different?

I learn to keep only three to five things in the fridge at any one time so that when I open it, I'm not overwhelmed. So that when I look, I see a meal to eat, not clusters of jars and bottles and bags. I cannot have boxes of cereal sitting cockeyed on top of the fridge, or bread things piled on the countertop, or a drawer full of cutlery and junk. If one thing is too far left or right, I can lose the whole day. Like a three-year-old, I need clean, conceptualized spaces with only one or two choices to select from. I've single-handedly created my own private Teletubbies world.

AND I HAD TO BE ALONE because anyone that came near me invaded me. Only in the absence of people could I boil myself down to a clear broth and add things a little at a time.

Occasionally I would venture out into the world with someone else as my escort, but it guaranteed nothing. Each random moment of interaction held danger.

I am in a bar with a new boyfriend, and growing jittery over the heaving crowd as the place starts to fill up. I hug the edges of the room, trying to stay untouched. My boyfriend catches my attention and waves me over. I follow, thinking he's got an island of safety for me to run to, but as I walk through the bar, the crowd closes in behind me. Boys in flannels are pressing against me, pushing in. Boys are clinking beer bottles over my head and laughing with sneaky, wily mouths. I flail and hit out wildly, trying to keep their breath from touching me, my hair slung over my face. My boyfriend is laughing. Laughing at how ridiculous I look; like I'm swatting at an imaginary swarm of bees. Every time I fly close to another's electrical line, I get a wing caught in the wire.

I HAVE LIVED MY LIFE IN A BUBBLE. First it was her bubble. Then it was of my own making. And now, freshly stripped of the delusions that had protectively swathed me for years, I was embryonic—too raw to interface directly with the world. People aren't just influential to me; a thin layer of them fuses onto me like hot cling wrap. Their words become my words, their voice inflections merge seamlessly into my own, their opinions form a transparency over the faint etchings of my own developing ones.

I look back through stacks of photographs of me after the fire. In each picture, I hold the facial tics and expressions of whoever I am involved with at the time. My face adopts the characteristics of the other, their fine lines, the exact way the jaw muscles freeze or flex within their smile. My face morphs to take on their identity.

Then I look at a baby picture of myself at six months old, lying on my belly, a natural smile lighting up my face. My own natural smile, unbroken, intact. This is the only picture I have of my own face, not someone else's. I wonder if I'm destined to drag around the past like a discarded placenta? I wonder how far do I boil back in order to reclaim my self? I ask how many pieces did I lose along the way? Where do I find them? Can I put them back? How many times do you glue a broken vase before you toss it?

I had been taken to the bone. My mother had fingered into me like the hollow of a melon and scooped me out. And now, years later, you could press belly to backbone.

Books are my friends, where it's okay to be silent, where you're not a freak if you don't want to get drunk, peel out in a parking lot, tip cows. Where it's okay to feel deeply, to languish, splashing and kicking in the deep end of the pool; even if I am all alone, and it's dark, after a big meal, with cramps, and I go under.

Books are what I'm bedding these days. When I'm not working at the clinic, all my time is spent slipped silently between their pages, finding some truth to go with the mirrors. They are self-help gurus who parent me positively and show me how to believe in myself. They suggest underlying spiritual philosophies: That each soul chooses its parents and all its experiences in order to learn the lessons it needs to develop fully. That if the soul's human form knew what it was supposed to learn beforehand, the ego would short-circuit the process of discovery. They tell me that, because of this double-blind experiment, where you find yourself in this painful process is exactly where you need to be.

That if you lived in a dark cave you'd need time to adjust to the light when the rock was rolled away.

That Hawaii had to be a volcanic eruption of toxic goo and ash before it became so lush and beautiful.

That if you watched the clothes in a washer, it would look like they're getting dirtier as they slosh through filthy water. But it's only after this *agitation* cycle that you can pull out fresh, clean clothes.

I bolster myself with platitudes: "We are who we are not despite adversity, but because of it" and "They say the truth hurts, but the only thing the truth hurts, are illusions." I sink the studs into soft dirt, and bank my new foundation.

My books talk to me like the child I am and coax me into developing autonomously. They metaphorically hang all the colored pictures I make on the fridge when I race home with them. They never tell me: *Lighten up, you think too much.* If anything, they say, *Hey, you, with the frontal lobe, turn off the TV, stop the noise, and consider this deeply.* They never dismiss me with *Get over it.* Or if I turn to my father: *What are you talking about?* My brother: *I don't remember anything.* Or my mother when I squeak out that I was too young to be taking a gun out of her mouth: "Jesus, Julie, where is a mother supposed to turn for support if not to her own daughter? You think the sun rises and sets on you, like you don't have any problems? I can think of a hundred times you . . ."

I pile my books around me before I sleep and they are the psychic guardrails that keep me from falling out of bed at night.

I DECIDE TO TRY OUT MY FATHER AGAIN, to see if I can reclaim one parent out of the whole mess. I could still run on one engine. Even though we have stayed in contact, our interactions skate on the thin ice of surface talk and carry us in awkward figure eights around each other. I cannot say that he even knows me as his daughter. Sometimes he calls me Sandy or Danny, like his father did to him, or hesitates altogether, trying to remember my name.

I meet him at the Chinese all-you-can-eat buffet of his choice and insist that it is only the two of us. He has already tried twice to cart along his girlfriend or Danny, anyone to maintain the space between us. I pull out a twenty-page letter on notebook paper that I have passionately penned the night before, telling him everything. He pulls out a pocket video game and begins to play solitaire.

"Dad," I say, leaning across the table, "did you know that Mom made things up about me?"

"Julie, you think you had it bad. Let me tell you something: When I was ten years old, just a little boy, I fell out the tree in the backyard. Chester was sitting in his chair watching TV. I had to carry my arm in there. I knew it was broken, and you know that bastard wouldn't even take me to the hospital until his show was over? My arm was broken and I had to wait a half hour to go to the hospital."

"Dad."

"Yeah, honey?"

"I broke both my arms and had to wait all day to go to the doctor."

"You broke your arm?" His brow furrows. "When?"

"Dad! When I was in second grade and then again in fourth grade. That time I had to wait until you came back from Burns Road to take me to Township. Don't you remember my casts?"

"Julie, I never knew you broke your arm."

At my prod, Dad reads the letter over his loaded plate. I am watching his face from across the table. From his expressions, I can follow the points in my letter; me telling him how much I loved him as a child, how he was my hero. And the loss I felt as he faded away and she got me all to herself. When he gets to the page where Mom slinks off to hide the tools that he is beating us for stealing, tears fall freely down his face and plop onto the greasy red-checkered tablecloth and I am crying with my father; we are reading the same letter, sitting across from each other, and it is the closest I've ever been to him. I am mesmerized by my father's tears; they are the tokens that will open him. I will turn to my father and catch the gold coins that pour from his heart like a slot machine and out into my open hands. I will scour my face with my golden hands and wash away the dirty tearstains of a trailer girl.

As he finishes, the same backlog of words, lost on my mother, are surging against my throat, to connect me to my father. This is the chance for us to lace back together and everything will be healed. I can barely wait for Dad to meet me after all this time. I have cracked him open and the reward will be mine.

Dad carefully folds my letter and stuffs it into his shirt pocket. "Shall we go, Sissy?"

Even better, he wants privacy. He doesn't want to address me in this chintzy place. In the parking lot, this is it, the moment, and I am walking along with him, breathing very, very still so that I won't miss a word, no matter how faint.

He clears his throat. "So, how's your car running?"

"Dad!"

"What?"

"What about the letter? What do you have to say about the letter? The letter, Dad?"

"Well, I've always told you I think your mother is sick. I'm sorry she did what she did."

"But Dad, you were a grown man, you have got to take responsibility for what you did, too! I mean, you made me eat Kleenex, Dad! For Christ's sake, you can't do that to a little girl! You have got to say you're sorry for the stuff you did as a grown man!"

"Well," Dad snorts, "I musta done something right! 'Cause you never left any snot rags lying around the house again, now, did you?"

TRUTH IS WHATEVER YOUR MIND BE-lieves. And beliefs are erected by those who raise us. If someone shapes your mind into a distortion, you have to find something that can give you the straight answer.

After that day with Dad, I knew that nobody could give me the straight answer but me. I used the mirrors to step back and forth between trips out into the real world, trips back into the swirling black hole of my family, trips to new ventures outside the bubble, seeing how long I could walk away from the mirror before the old thoughts submerged the fresh ones. Sometimes I'd only get to the kitchen or down a few steps of the porch. Sometimes, I could make it half a day before I'd have to rush back to see myself.

As summer comes, I build on my new foundation, gaining momentum. I frisk and rub my skin, trying to jumpstart my appetite. I knead fingers into my flesh and pound my legs with my fists, to stimulate withered muscles. I use baths to alter my physical experience and break my time into more manageable chunks that structure the day.

My "To Do" list reads: get up, wash hair, eat. Each time I finish something from my list I cross it out and feel the dizzy thrill of accomplishment. And every so often, I catch a glimpse of myself while walking past a mirror and my face snaps into recognizing the beauty I see before me. My smile comes more natural, without the chunky mental gap in catching myself up with what I see. Each flash in the mirror strings along my self-continuity like individual Styrofoam packing peanuts, making a colorful second-grade party decoration I tack up over the fading past.

With my freshly wired instincts, I inch farther and farther out of my incubator. I stay longer in the real world and run back with less frenzy when waves begin crashing. When I do slip under, I whip out a pen and write myself back to the surface, using whatever material I can snatch up to capture the barrage: bar napkins, toilet paper, airline barf bags, my bare leg. I scribble my thoughts and tweak them with words from my new vocabulary. I talk myself out of paranoia and coax myself from ledges. I fill volumes of journal books with these moments; packed with crowded text, both sides scribbled and stuffed with snippets of paper, smeary inked paper towels, feverishly written.

My life is now lived in triplicate: one life in the mirror, one in the world, and one balancing the two as oceans which must wax and wane in tandem until one replaces the other.

I HAVE ACQUIRED ONE PURPLE YOGA MAT, my first instrument of health. I lie on it and roll around like an undernourished weeble-wobble, doing my own pathetic version of whatever exercises I can think of. I gradually work up to riding a bicycle, an ancient green Schwinn, my lucky number 7 painted on its lug-heavy frame. I manage short spurts at first, down the alley and back, around the block, and eventually I coast down small hills and chug back up at a snail's pace, puffing and panting in the August heat. My legs buzz with circulation. There is a current running through me, a current of life, of electricity, of excitement, a vague sense of health, like I could almost reach out and grasp it and tug it toward me before it dissipates. I strip off my clothes and look at my body in the mirror. It is transforming before my eyes. Each day I seem to grow by leaps and bounds; my hair, my height, I catch a faint shadow of muscle outlining my leg, my blue veins gone, gorged and drunk on the blood I've surged through them.

I sit in the lounge area of my first gym, filling out membership forms. One reads:

Have you ever been on any medication?
Have you ever had a heart problem?
Shortness of breath?
Chest pain?
Any hospitalizations?
Surgeries?
History of medical problems?
Are you allergic to anything?
If yes to any, please explain.

How do you explain? The lines at the bottom aren't long enough. And if the answers to those questions were "yes" in my past, and that past was a lie, does that mean they really happened with enough validity to mark them now with a "yes"? What they are looking for are legitimate medical problems, but I don't have any. Right?

With black pen in hand, I zip through the questionnaire, carving a solid black NO in every column.

IT IS ONE DREAMY NIGHT and I am on my way to court a boy as sensitive and in need of protection as I am. He is my age and he is delicate and beautiful. The urge to be with him is enough to break me out of the safe ten-mile radius from home. The moon is huge and silvery, hanging in a gray winter sky as the city lights fade behind me and I head out to the country. And now I am passing

Township Family Physicians where it all began. I have not seen its single-story nondescript edifice for ten years, and I have not thought about it once in all the time since I learned what it spawned in my life. I push down on the accelerator and race past it, as if Township could reach out and grab me if I don't make it quick. I drive to my boy's house and fall into his arms as the story exits me, for the first time understood; rough stones gone into the tumbler, smooth articulated gems fall from my mouth.

And from there, I gather the courage to call Township for my medical file. I am ready to see what they saw and strong enough in the truth of what really happened to read my records without derailing. I go to pick them up and wait in the lobby where I sat all those afternoons as a girl. A television runs a loop of commercials promoting medications and medical procedures as if they were spa treatments: happy people in pastels running through fields, looking over their shoulders and laughing.

Then I begin tracing the other places where my mother had taken me. Some doctors were dead, some had moved, the surgeon who did my nose job left town without a forwarding address. There were many one-time appointments where I could not remember the location or the name of the doctor. I was only nine, ten, eleven. Sometimes we traveled an hour to get me to a new physician. If we hit a dead end, there was no reason to return. Or forward records. Leaving behind the ones that said I was normal was as easy as not giving a forwarding address.

The records poured in. As soon as I'd get a packet, I'd sit down wherever I was and rip open the envelope. A hundred and fifty pages of wasted time. A hundred and fifty pages of lost innocence.

Department of Medicine
Cardiology

July 6, 1984

Dr.

Re: Julia Gregory

Dear Dr.

I saw Julie Gregory this morning in the clinic and find her doing
extremely well. She wanted to double her 25 mgm dose of atenolol
taken as bid, and I wasn't opposed to this although wanted to recheck
her systolic intervals and echocardiogram before doing so. She
continues to have particularly exercise-related rapid heart action,
and I therefore rechecked her thyroid function tests and CBC wanting
to exclude contributors to the hyperdynamic circulatory state.

Her EKG is as before and still shows small subtle delta waves and
borderline shortening of the PR interval. Unless there is some
striking finding in her noninvasive data, I would feel comfortable in
her doubling her present dose of beta blockade.

Her mother had questions about school-related travel this summer, and
I see no real reason to limit this patient's activities.

I'll see her again in a year with your permission.

Sincerely,

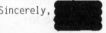

, M.D.
Division of Cardiology

Enclosures

IN THE RECORDS ON MY HEART CATHETERIZATION is a letter written by my childhood cardiologist. It's from a follow-up visit when I was fifteen.

You were a grown man, an experienced doctor. How could you have missed it? What fifteen-year-old goes to the cardiologist to discuss her dose of Atenolol?

You as a doctor are an authority on human behavior; able to smell a rat and ferret out a liar. Do you think I perhaps had other things to do as a fifteen-year-old than come to your office? Are you sure it wasn't possibly my mother who made the appointment? Who spoke to you about new symptoms, who told you I had asked her if you would amp-up my medication? Who leaned forward on the edge of her chair and cocked her head to discuss the dangers of a young heart patient traveling that summer, or doing sports, or having friends? And is it possible that you are the same doctor who stood in the hallway just two years earlier and firmly told my mother to drop the quest for the holy-grail heart operation? And now you sit discussing calmly with her my wish to double my heart medication?

Hmmm, I thought so.

THE MEEK CHILD WITH A HEART CONDITION has died. I am a real woman now, with a woman's body and temperament. I can articulate my thoughts, feelings, wants and desires. I stand tall in the grocery store. I talk to people without bolting. I interact with men as a woman, not as a doe in season. And as my docility turns to dust, I have the growing undeniable awareness of something very evil and dark surging against the inside of my skin, trying to claw its way out.

My rage is unstoppable. It vomits out of me; I tear

the head off of store clerks, telephone operators, anyone too slow to stop me. I am meticulous and merciless. They are all incompetent. They are all stupid. They are all worthless. I want to beat them with the flyswatter. I crash hours after my blinded frenzy with the insight of what I am doing: making someone pay, just like my mother made me pay, just like she made the foster kids pay, just like she made the doctors pay; unleashing fury on any person too scrambled by the attack to call her on it. And now I want to make people feel bad, extract guilt with precision instruments and fillet another's self-confidence, just as I saw my mother do to the doctors who saw me. I have got to stop.

IN SHEN THERAPY, you climb into a cloth bed that is slung up on a tabletop as a hammock. It's suspended in a dim, peaceful room and the SHEN practitioner does a gentle placement of her hands just above the body, mostly hovering around the stomach, where nerves that run between your sternum and your pelvis lock emotional trauma. The SHEN practitioner then guides you into deep breathing, while she tries to unblock the emotions. Judith, the therapist, has asked me to commit to two months of sessions. After our consultation, she decides to give them to me, free of charge.

Lying in the SHEN cocoon, I slip into a deep state. We are halfway through our weeks and I am opening in ways that defy my skepticism. I am floating under Judith's hands and she is warm, serene, and all-encompassing. I have never felt safer. Our sessions are usually silent, but today she has me visualize where I was the first time I felt something wasn't right.

I remember. I see a little girl with short choppy hair. My fists grip. The little girl is clutching a flyswatter. A smile curls her mouth, just like her mother's.

"I see her."

"How old is she, Julie?"

My eyes squeeze tight trying to stop the sight of her.

"She's eleven," I growl. "I can't stand her!"

"Why don't you like her, when she's that young?"

"She beat those kids, she beat those kids till they screamed. I hate her. I want to kill her." I'm starting to hyperventilate.

"Okay, Julie, let's let go of her. Let's slow down the breath."

"I hate her. Judith, I hate her!"

"Okay, let it go. Is she gone?"

My breathing slows.

"Now I want you to fast forward to a later age. How old were you the next time you knew?"

I'm in the bottom bunk bed of Danny's room. I can hear them through the thin trailer walls. "Oh, my God. I was twelve. Mom and Dad were in bed at night and they were fighting over me, over what they were going to do to me. I wanted to take a kitchen knife and stick it in my gut before they did."

"So you can see this girl and she is twelve. And she is there in the bunk bed. You are there standing in her room, looking at her. What do you want to say to this girl?"

"Say? I'm not going to say anything to her! I've got to get her out of there, Judith! Those people are crazy. I can't let her stay there. They'll destroy her. I have to take her now. Now, not wait for some pansy-assed caseworker to drift around trying to find an undetectable poison. I have to get her out, Judith. I have to take her!"

"Okay, so get her out of there. Scoop her up and run out of there. Now you are out. She is with you and you are living safe, years later. What are you going to say to her?"

"Oh, Judith," my head flops to the side and I beam into the dark room, "she is so precious; every day I'm going to tell her how she's beautiful and how much I love her and how I'm so sorry for everything she went through and I promise I'll make it up to her in love. And she is going to grow up to be the most loved little girl ever and she will heal. They'll never get her again."

That was where SHEN took me.

I NOW FEEL READY to try a talk therapist again. Most times I do not feel like a client, but an educator who pays to teach my therapist about MBP. I answer her questions: How did it slip past doctors? Why didn't anybody notice? Didn't you have any neighbors? Were you really sick?

But still, in our sessions, I cry from the guilt of betraying my mother, for not keeping the shroud on her secrets when I held them locked in such trust. And I feel terrible about my own secret. I have been writing, writing about what it feels like to be cut open while your mother's tight, thin smile mouths, *"Doctor's orders, honey."* To be emptied and filled by your mother, just like the IV bag she's arranged for you. And to believe you are genuinely ill because that is what everything in your world mirrors back to you.

My therapist explains that in her opinion my mother was cannibalistic. That she wanted to ingest my living flesh, to tear chunks from my body. That the closest she could come to cannibalizing me was to lift me onto the serving platter for the men of the medical community to carve. The longer I hold guilt for betraying her, the more I will keep climbing on the platter all by myself.

And yet the hand that pushed me down was the hand that helped me up. The one who beat me was the only one who could save me from being beaten. The one who wanted to kill me was the one who would kill herself if I didn't offer myself under the knife. I was trained from the womb as an alibi to her innocence. She would snuff out my life if I went against her, even in thought. She brushed me this way as casually as you would slide a lint brush down a pair of slacks, to get all the grain running the same direction.

I still told myself that it was okay, it really wasn't that bad. A normal sacrifice for any child to make for her mother. Words programmed into me as my own. Tangled in her web, if a doctor couldn't decipher what she did, how could I?

UNTIL I TURN THIRTY. Then I see her almost as clearly as if I was standing on a wind-swept sea cliff and she was looking up from the sand below. There is only one line that connects us, and it is wrapped around my waist; my hunger is tied to the most intimate, emotionally deep contact you can ever get: a mother's touch. Anything less than where she took me feels like not enough.

And so it is for the people I bring into my life. My relationships, like the one I had with my mother, turn immediately intense, sometimes violently invasive. I start to see that I surround myself with broken people; more broken than me. Ah, yes, let me count your cracks. Let's see, one hundred, two . . . yes, you'll do nicely. A cracked companion makes me look whole, gives me something outside myself to care for. When I'm with whole, healed people I feel my own cracks; the shatters, the insanities of dislocation in myself.

So I start over. When I ruin something or when someone vines around me, I move on. It is just another opportunity, another chance to interact with the outside world and not have it take me completely, utterly, to the bone.

I am leaving Ohio. My farmhouse is being torn down; its south side is sliding into the ravine below. I take a mallet to the wall that used to hold my largest mirror and haul my arm back, again and again, bellowing out the names of anything or anyone who ever hurt me. Holes open in the plaster and swallow sheets of ancient wallpaper. I build a pyre in the backyard and toss in the emergency boxes of cake batter, page after page of duplicate medical records, college papers with As and Fs, letters from boys, letters from men, piles of belongings that never fit, not then, not now—all the things I've collected and clung to since the first fire ripped away everything I'd ever loved.

The singed ashes waft up, up, high into the night sky, just as I used to envision my body, thin and brittle as a maple leaf. I close the back door on my empty farmhouse, now as devoid of life as the crisp locust shell left behind after the metamorphosis. I load my guitar and a paper bag full of clothes in my old convertible and pull out at midnight with a sack of vegetables and juice. I am driving clean and clear to Los Angeles, where you can start over on a daily basis, where you can be anonymous for life, where you can dissolve into a sea of people, and no one could care less if you lived or died on the sidewalk.

AND WITH EACH MILE THAT TICKS on my odometer, my memory of my mother falls away just a little more, broken cliffs dropping off into the depths of memory. Like the shopping stops we made after my doctors' appointments that severed me from what had really happened earlier that day, the quick and abrupt changes I take in life place me that much further from trusting my memories of the past. And the more I acclimate to the normal world, the more and more surreal and unbelievable the world I came from seems.

I'd lived through it without anyone seeing it. Then I'd untangled from it without anyone confirming it. Now, years later and thousands of miles away, little rays of doubt were beginning to sliver my thoughts.

Surely she had never been all that bad. Surely by now, she had changed. She did what she did because she needed to. She reenacted it on me, just like an abused kid would do with a doll. Now that it was over, I was sure she'd be a whole different person.

This is how I led myself back. Because the more I changed my scenery, the more I gave away. The more I gave away, the more I needed. The more I needed, the more I pined for a mother, a mother to help me, a mother to belong to. I desperately searched the eyes of other mothers, hungering to be embraced as a little girl—just what my mother wanted from me. I longed to lay my head in a mother's lap. I soothed myself to sleep during middle-of-the-night panics by imagining a kind, soothing mother sitting on the edge of my bed, hand slowly caressing strands of my hair, curling it behind my ears, around her fingers, sinking me dreamy with electric pulses that dropped like shooting stars across my scalp. Healing my skull with the heat of her hands.

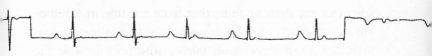

I HAVE NOT SEEN HER in seven years. Our last photograph was taken on Mother's Day with the two of us sitting on a log somewhere out in the woods on a trail ride, eating pack lunches and smiling for the camera, Mom's brassy hair glinting in the sun from a fresh scrubbing of bleach.

A few months later I would be crumpled at the bottom of a stairwell, my life charred to nothing, and she would be on her way to Montana, leaving her nothing life behind, to start over. Now, so far away from my past and changing my life every six months, I have rummaged through my memories and selected the tiniest shards of our life together to reconstruct an apparition; bending or soldering strands of memory to erect a motherly hologram that wavers just out of reach, beckoning to me.

ONE AFTERNOON WHEN I AM THIRTY-ONE, I hold my breath and dial her number.

"Sandy?" I could not bring myself to mouth *Mom*. "Hi. It's Julie."

I am expecting nothing, anger maybe, or a tidal wave of guilt from her.

"Sis? Oh, my God, Julie, it's so good to hear your voice. Where are you? I've been worried sick."

And so it began, the gradual reopening to my mother. After several smooth phone calls, in which I deny her my own number each time she asks, I eventually wear down and give her a way to reach me. She promises she'll never call too late, her own unspoken apology for all those middle-of-the-night suicide calls she used to make.

LOS ANGELES IS A LONELY PLACE. Being anonymous gets tiring. In Ohio I stood out; in L.A., everyone is different. You can never be enough for L.A. People you give your phone number to never call you. The more you hunger for contact, the less you get. People can smell need in Los Angeles, and they stay away.

By default, my mother became my one lifeline back to people more solid, who weren't washed away every twenty-four hours by the tide. I told her my woes of life in a big empty city.

"You can always come home, Sis."

Home, Sis. The concept of flying off to live with my mother seemed absurd. But I was so tired of my independence, turning myself over to be taken care of by her had daydreamy high points.

Over the year, Mom sent me boxes of things I needed but didn't have the extra money to buy. When my car got clamped, she sent me the check to get it out of the clink. She helped me at my lowest points and, for the first time, she was my mom. I didn't need to save her. I needed her and she was saving me, saying all the right words to support me, calling at all the right times. My wariness evaporated. *She's changed, she's trying to make it up to me, we don't even need to talk about what happened, just her reaching out is enough.*

S ANDY IS COMING TO GET ME in Great Falls, Montana. I have little money and fewer plans. I was going to write a book about my life with her, but I need my mother more.

I have to know: know if she really can be the mom in person that she is on the phone—or have I just filled in the blanks with false hope?

She has a little farmhouse on the lot next to hers she is going to give me so I can rest and put down some roots. I will live there with my little dog LuLu, and all will be well in my life because I will have a mother at last.

It takes three planes to get to Montana, each of them growing successively smaller, like the doorways of Alice in Wonderland, until the last plane dips through the empty sky like a pop can on a kite string.

I come off the ramp at the tiny Great Falls airport, laden with belongings for my new life; my little dog in a leopard-print shoulder bag, clothes, books. I spot my mother.

My God, life has been hard to her.

I barely recognize her. She certainly doesn't look capable of her past or mine. Her face seems swollen, as if a toxic buildup has been brewing under her skin. Standing behind her is a small cluster of people she calls her family, who she introduces as her husband Ed and their two small adopted children, Tina and Paul. I swallow.

We bunch up under the stuffed airport grizzly, sadly positioned on its hind legs to look menacing, and Ed snaps a picture. Mom tells the children to smile and they beam just as we used to do, while she cocks her leg like a model's, just like always.

We load up in the family minivan for the hundred miles to their remote cattle ranch. On the way, Mom wants to stop at Ponderosa Steakhouse to celebrate. As we sit around a wood-veneered diner table, the ice slowly starts to melt. I am the grown adult daughter and this is my mother's new life. I have come here to slip into it, and I am willing it to work out for all of us.

Over our steak dinners and tin-foiled baked potatoes, I eye Tina carefully. She is eleven and her brother, Paul, is four, the same age difference as Danny and me. She is small, like I was, and she wears her hair in the same ridiculous shag my mother gave me when she lopped off my waist-length locks. Fiddling with my meal, I am watching my mother between the blinds, looking in the spaces between her words as she talks to Tina and Paul, seeing if she still is the woman of my childhood.

But she isn't.

Everything goes well, the kids laugh, she and Ed seem to be stable. She has a big wedding ring on her finger. When we finally get to the house, the kids pull out presents for me and squeal, "Will you be our big Sissy?" while Mom hauls out a cake with candles from the kitchen. I have never known such welcome from my family before. I am moved. We all crowd together by the refrigerator and set the auto timer on the Kmart camera. The hugs and affection make me tear up right there at the kitchen table—the same fake wood-look kind that I sat at all those nights back in Ohio, talking with my mother. I am looking forward to being wrong. I am looking forward to tearing up the writings that would haunt me; haunt me like hell if I could ever call her "Mom" once again.

She has made me my very own room, with an electric blanket because she knows I get cold at night, with extra pillows to tuck between my knees. She has laid out the best towels. She shows me where everything is and treats me like a guest. She has bought me some clothes and given me new sheets, in spring colors she's hoping I'll like. I climb in bed like a child and bring myself to mouth what I could not say for seven years.

"Good night," it sticks in my throat, so out of practice, "Mom."

She turns out the light. "Nighty-night, Sis."

I sleep like a baby.

THE NEXT MORNING, the house is up early. Mom and Ed are outside working and the kids sit at the table, hunched over bowls of Sugar Snaps.

Today I tour the farm. The house Mom and her family live in is a cleverly concealed double-wide trailer, thanks to various add-ons, cute country throw rugs, and a concrete porch goose dressed in gingham. The kids' rooms are stocked with toys and movies. Tina has a canopy bed done up in pastels, just like I did. Paul sleeps in a bed shaped like a race car. It all looks good.

But I start to notice other details. Mom's shoes have multiplied by the hundreds and are brutally stuffed into large storage boxes, their toes and heels jutting desperately from the hand slots and out from under the cheap cardboard lids, as if gasping for breath. The boxes are stacked haphazardly upon one another. And still more shoes: piled into black garbage bags, tossed into the tack sheds and pull-behind trailers that scatter the yard.

Neighbors are nonexistent. The land they live on spans hundreds of acres, and though the house sits on the edge of it by the road, miles run between them and any other home. The slaughterhouse horses of my time are now fat-bellied Paints and breeding mares. Their heat cycles mark the calendar that hangs in the kitchen, and babies are always on the verge of being born and being sold. They need buckets of grain, bales of hay, hours of work. Everything else in the day is secondary. The school Tina attends has a total of eight students, spanning kindergarten through the sixth grade. I wonder how a child could learn anything in such a limited and contained setting. One man serves as principal, custodian, and teacher. In the summers, during school break, he doubles as a big-rig truck driver.

Later over dinner, we inch into one another carefully, trying to pull our worlds, as fragile and shiny as Christmas bulbs, together, without breaking them. Paul babbles incoherently at the table and Mom strains to address everything he says with patience and a smile, to show how she's changed. Tina is unusually quiet for a girl of eleven. I want to draw her out and see if she comes with me.

"So, Tina, what are you up to in school?"

Tina pivots her face to my mother, who answers without looking at her. "Well, Tina's slow, she's got fetal alcohol syndrome. She does okay in school, but she's not going to get past a certain grade level. She was in bad shape when she came here, weren't you, Tina?"

"Uh-huh, Mom."

"But she's doing real good now. Right, honey?"

Tina nods. I cannot seem to finish my pot roast. And

neither does Tina. She scoots it around her plate, resting her head on a back-flipped wrist, and dismisses herself with an apologetic "I don't really like meat."

That night, Mom and I sit at the kitchen table and talk, just like we used to, but with me on the outside now, hoping to lay to rest the small fracture that formed at the dinner table.

She is talking about old times with Smokey and how my birthday falls on their wedding anniversary. Each May sixteenth, she cannot reach me because I have buried myself in the world, and she cannot reach him because he is simply buried. And she is talking about her new life here, how good a man Ed is if only by the qualifier that he doesn't beat her like my father did. In her eyes, she's moved up. He has a brother, you know, good man, wants a wife and kids; she showed him my picture. Sure would like to meet me while I'm here. And she relaxes into telling me of the day-to-day life she lives now, here on the vast plains of Montana.

"We drove through two creeks with no bridges to get on this pack trip and ride over the Continental Divide from Palookaville. We musta been thirty miles into that trail ride when Jonas Walker's horse got flanked and commenced to bucking. Bucked him headfirst into some rocks and broke his neck and killed him. That's the first year we ever carried a cell phone, being out in the high country. Now, Jonas was a white man befriended by the Indian, very loved by the Indians, by the Sioux tribe, and they held ceremony for him high on a hill overlooking the twin rivers, Indian ceremony, you know. They summoned the spirits, they did their drumming, and my God, a couple of eagles started flying overhead and I got chills all over."

These are the stories I like to hear most from my

mother, told in the cadence of old-time gospel or the slow, pausing pace of a good Indian story. They are never about my father or the hard life she's lived, but of the events that give her goose bumps or awe her in heart or spirit. In these small silent moments, waiting for a pause to pass, I notice her hands, swollen and knotty, from a self-imposed sentence of hard labor. One of her fingers has been sewn on at the knuckle; it flips out sideways from the rest.

"So, Mom, how's your health been?"

"My God, Julie, I am just about sicker than a dog most of the time. Look at this thing." She lugs up her shirt to expose a thick raised scar running across her back from her armpit to her bottom. It looks like a mole has burrowed diagonally across her ribs. "This one nearly killed me. They sawed my ribs out and nearly cut into my spine, my discs was fused together."

I cannot get a straight answer as to why, exactly, she had to have this serious surgery. But it was due to the incompetence of these country bumpkin doctors out here, she says, that her finger got stitched on backwards. Another time, she goes on, her eyelids got laced with the toxic powder from an incandescent lightbulb when she went to change it and it burst in its socket. And just this past year, she has been seeing cardiologists.

"They got me wearing something called a Holter monitor." She articulates this slowly to make sure I can follow. "That's one of those things they make you wear so they can monitor your heart at home. I asked my doctor what's the worse-case scenario here? A bypass? Open-heart? Tell me what the damage might be, just so I know. You know?"

Blood drains from me. I look around the kitchen

while she talks. Her hutch is lined with hardcover medical books and thick pill-identification guides. Medication bottles cluster on the ledge beside the microwave and cover a plate that sits on top of the fridge.

"She said they might have to do this invasive procedure they call a heart cath—that's, you know, cardio terminology—if I get any more of these episodes here at home."

I grip my cold fingertips to the bottom of the chair. I lead the conversation back to Tina.

"Oh, Julie, that little girl came out of the most god-awful situation you could imagine. Her dad's in jail, mom's a drug addict, and that's what's wrong with her, see, she was born slow, she's got that fetal alcohol thingy that makes kids small, you know? And she has just done great since she's been here. She tested at first-grade level, but she's come a long, long way. She's so happy now. I know we've had our past and all the hard times with your father, but now that I'm away from him, I'm a better person. You just watch, you'll see."

"Yeah, Mom, I believe you."

THE NEXT MORNING, while Mom is outside watering her plants, I brown sixteen breakfast sausages and scramble eggs. It's just me and Tina in the kitchen and the sausages don't even make it to the table. She scarfs them off the paper towels as I lift one after another from the griddle to the plate. I pull her over to me and show her step by step how to make them; medium heat, turn them over and over till they're brown on all sides. I stick the spatula in her hand and stand behind her, blocking the view of her in case someone comes in. There is a charged electricity in the air: We are conspiring against Sandy;

we are doing something wrong. We both jump in our skin when Mom rushes through the screen door.

"Tina, goddammit, you know better than to use the stove! How many times have I told you, you are not allowed to cook!"

I interrupt her. "Sandy, I'm showing Tina how to make sausages so she can feed herself if she's hungry. She's going to be tall and skinny. She could use some protein in the morning."

"What are you trying to say, Julie? That I don't feed the girl? That girl can eat whenever, whatever she likes. We got a whole refrigerator full of food." Tina stands frozen, holding the spatula in midair.

"But kids can't just eat sugary cereal for breakfast. Tina can learn to use the stove to fix sausage when she wants to."

"Julie, you just keep your nose out of this. That girl knows she ain't supposed to turn the stove on. Don't you, Tina, you know that, right? She's slow, you got it? She'll burn the house down."

Slow, as in I was slow, as in I would never get past a certain intelligence level, either. Burn the house down, as in what you and Pop did to get the insurance money— but nobody else knows that, so it would be a perfectly reasonable concern to tell people since you lost your home once, why take chances again? This is the advanced logic all those years in isolation granted me, the clarity to smell, see, and taste an undetectable poisonous gas.

TINA STAMMERS HER APOLOGY to Mom and tries to duck down the hall. I am careening backwards, into some magnetic swirling time warp, powerless against my mother. I can only witness what's unfolding.

Mom calls, "Tina, get back here, did we give you your medication today?" Mom is grabbing vials off the fridge and slamming pills into her palm. "Well, here, let's make sure you get them now."

She slaps the drugs in Tina's hand. The child swallows without blinking.

My stomach is reeling, I vomit in the bath. This can't be happening. Not me, all over again. Tina is eleven, the same age as the girl I visualized in SHEN therapy.

What are you going to say to her, Julie?

I'm not going to say anything. I've got to get her out of there.

"LET'S JUST GET ONE THING STRAIGHT, you are not going to come into my house and tell me how to raise these kids, all right? Now you look like hell—If anyone knows what healthy is, it's not you. You are not going to turn that girl against me."

The rest of the day is spent on pins and needles, tiptoeing around my mother. On my end I am trying to calm her so I can gain her trust and gather details on Tina: doctors' names, medical history, Tina's real last name so I can trace her at the adoption agency. Everyone else is trying to calm her so she doesn't fly off the handle. It is a project that involves the whole family.

Ed catches me in the barn. "Uh, Julie, could I just have a little word with you? Your mom treats them kids good. She's always feedin' them and buying them clothes. She may get a little upset about Tina not doing good in school, but she's always treating them real good."

I can hear Mom in the kitchen, hissing to Tina, "Go tell her, Tina, get in there and tell her." And Tina trots in to corner me at the freezer. "Julie. I love my mommy.

She feeds me and treats me real good." Tina is automated, just like I was.

The more I try to de-escalate the sausage incident, the more my mother amps up the volume. I have plucked her rawest nerve, challenged her in her most primal identity: her ability to mother. And I have revealed that I know her tried and true secret for lacing up an appendage, keeping a child bound.

She spends the day huffing and cursing, following me through the trailer. That night, after the kids have gone to bed, she corners me. "Okay now, we're going to sit down here and get through this once and for all. Ed, you get in here. I want you to listen to this!"

"Sandy, I really don't think this is necessary. I don't want to make you any angrier."

"Oh, no. Oh, no, you don't, you're not going to get out of this one, young lady. You get your ass in here and talk to us like an adult. Now what the hell is wrong with you? Why are you doing this to me?"

"Sandy, really, I don't think . . ." I'm trailing off, but isn't this what I've waited for? Haven't I wanted the lead-in to tell her all these years? Haven't I wanted the satisfaction of telling her what she did? Deep breath. I can do it. "Okay. Sandy, when I was a little girl, well. Okay. Well, you did things to me when I was a kid and I see the same patterns being repeated with Tina."

My mother's eyes narrow to slits. "Let me tell you something, girl, that kid is a moron, she does terrible in school, she will never amount to anything, and if I didn't take her in, nobody would, you got that? Nobody would have that son-of-a-bitchin' girl!"

"Sandy, this is exactly what I'm saying. You said the same things about me! That I was stupid, that I would never amount to anything, that I had something wrong with me that would keep me held back my whole life."

"Ed. You want to help me here? You just going to sit there and let her talk to me that way? Aren't you going to be a man and get involved here and stand up for me?"

"Well, Sandy, she ain't saying nothing 'gainst you, just that you did things to her that she don't think was right and she thinks you're doing them to Tina. Well, that's just in her opinion."

"Oh. My. God. I don't believe this. So that's what this is all about!" My mother is escalating into hysterics. The realization of stumbling upon something dark and terrible clouds her face. "I'll be goddamned." She is dumbfounded, astonished. "You came out here to steal my husband! You and him got something going on together, now, don't you?" She slaps her leg in revelation. "Oh, Jesus, I shoulda known I couldn't trust you." Her brain is tallying the impact of my affair with Ed at lightning speed and she shrieks, "You can have her, Ed, you can shack up with her and I'll just crawl off and die." It's one in the morning and she is storming through the rooms, flailing her arms and launching at things to throw while Ed tries to calm her from his armchair.

"Just leave me alone," she screams. "You and her can just run off together, the two of you, and I'll just stay here and kill myself!"

And she has won. She is racing back to her bedroom where the shotgun leans against their wall. She is going to take the gun and Ed is going to save her. She is manufacturing the glue that will bond the two of them back together and seal her cracks in the process. And no one will call her on it because she has made them responsible for whether she commits suicide or not. Tonight will never be mentioned again. It is not about Tina or what Mom did to me. It is not about the sausages or the starving or the pursuit of sickness and surgery. It will be remembered as the time I tried to break up her marriage to a good man.

I run into my room and wedge a chair under the doorknob. She screams hysterically and races through the trailer, while Ed tries to wrestle the shotgun away from her. I brace my back against the door in panic, my breath coming in gasps. It is not my place to go out there and take the gun from her. It is not my responsibility to save her. And there is a new awareness tonight, something I have never known before; a strong inkling that we have grown so separate, so distant and distinct from one another, my mother and I, that the gun she's charging around with might not be for her after all, but for me.

THE NEXT MORNING, Ed drives me to the airport. I'm shell-shocked. I have made it three days with my mother. I am carting back the dog, the clothes, the books. The presents stay behind, the cake overturned and smeared into the kitchen's indoor-outdoor carpet. As we pull out of the driveway, Sandy is sitting in the minivan at the end of the lane with Tina. She does not want to even be in the same house as me, the home-wrecker. She wants to watch Ed from afar and be witness to him cheating on her. And Tina, like I was, is the therapist she leans on.

On the hour-and-a-half drive, I learn that Ed is not an actual husband. Sandy bought the ring herself and started using his last name a few years ago. The stones are cubic zirconia. The children are not adopted. They are distant relatives twice removed from Ed's side, and after they'd been shuffled around to other family members that didn't want them, Mom jumped on the chance to get them.

Ed says, "You know, your mother just gets like this sometimes and the only thing you can do is agree with her and try to calm her down." If only you knew, Ed.

But he doesn't. Sandy is Ed's first real girlfriend. Ed has lived as a Montana cattle rancher his whole life, too remote even for *Sweethearts Magazine*. He lived with his parents until he was in his thirties, until Sandy met him at a barn dance. Ed and I share the same decade. Just as my mother shares the same decade with his. And Ed wouldn't recognize child abuse if it slapped him upside the head.

He drops me off at the airport and we exchange clunky good-byes. He's sorry it didn't work out between us. Sandy sure was looking forward to having me around; she's got too much work with them horses to have that girl be doing it all by herself.

"I know, Ed. I know."

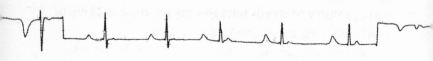

W HEN I WRITE IT ALL OUT, I just fall
over asleep. It plucks the stuffing right
out of me, like pulling the marrow from my bones. I'm
good for about an hour and then I cut off into dreamless, flat sleep, drugged by the arrow tips of memory that
slip poison into my bloodstream.

All I want to do while I write is lie in bed and be a
hospital patient. I don't want to talk to anybody. I don't
want to see anybody. But I don't want to be alone, either. I want people bustling somewhere off in the distance, doing the things that keep them busy, but nearby
in case I need them. Writing about my life is like pulling
a fine hair out the back of my throat. I just keep pulling
and pulling and it just keeps coming. It's exhausting. So
I rest. Some days I stay in bed all day, write, sleep. Sometimes I go out and come back, write, sleep. Sometimes I
sleep when I write and sometimes I write when I sleep.
When I write about pushing a gun into Dad's head, I
close my eyes and slip into a blank dreamless void. I
come to an hour later, my fingertips still touching the

keys. When I sleep, I write perfectly formed text directly from a deep place, without the use of my hands or mouth, because something gets lost in the transmission. I see the text before me: exactly what I mean to convey, in its purest form—indents of paragraphs, brushstrokes of feeling. I am flushed with the beauty of it. When I wake, a flurry of words operates my hands, a backlog of words building inside, rushing to get out.

I WAKE IN THE NIGHT to panicked dreams of Tina in Montana. My heart thuds densely in my chest. What am I doing here? I have to get her out. I can't just sit around and pretend it didn't happen and isn't getting worse every day. I have to get her out.

But I am petrified of my mother. While I sat in the Great Falls airport, waiting for the next flight out, she called everyone she had a phone number for and told them about my trouble with the police, you know, that warrant out for my arrest. I came back to L.A. to find a voice mailbox full of messages from people who know me, but don't know Sandy. From people who have normal moms and dads, who can't comprehend the lengths a biological mother will go to discredit her offspring and bolster her own cemented denial.

I know that if I call Montana Children's Services and they send a caseworker out, my mother will know it was me. That she will at first feign shock, then chuckle as she puts the pieces together in front of the caseworker and it dawns on her, that, oh, this must be the work of my homeless daughter. She will dab at a few tears and explain the story of her oldest daughter who has been in and out of mental hospitals. It will be far easier for the Montana caseworker to believe that, than to look around at the pastel rooms full of toys and stuffed animals and detect the subtle odor of poisonous gas.

I know Tina will answer all the questions to benefit my mother, because she's been told that if they take her away she'll be raped. I know Ed will be himself, a good-hearted, painfully naïve ranch boy. I know that Paul will cling to my mother's leg and wail, "Mommmmyy." I know that the case will get dismissed and my mother will simply tighten her security on the kids or even worse, move them to a place where I'll lose all ability to check on them. I have got to do this right. I have got to go back to Ohio, the heart of it all. And I have got to be as crafty as my own Munchausen by proxy mother.

DANNY PICKS ME UP AT THE AIRPORT. We are happy enough to see each other but we don't have much to say. It's been two years since he's seen me and even longer since he's seen Sandy. His memory, as mine once did, has opted for the starrier picture. It was just last year, when Danny was twenty-four, that the only thing he wanted for Christmas was a tape of Mom's singing, one of the few good things strained from our life with her.

He still needs a mom and dad. His psyche has draped the sharp edges of detail in a thick drop cloth as he keeps the past at bay with workaholism and asthma attacks that coincide with Mom's random phone calls to him. He is a race car driver, a full-time engineer, a restorer of vintage cars—anything to gobble up the seconds in his day and direct his thoughts into a plan for the future. He owns a home and acreage, a John Deere tractor, and fifty classics waiting to be fixed, ticking in his head for every moment he can't get to them. And to me he feels far older than the youth of his actual years.

I am a writer with nothing but endless interior corridors in which to wander. I own almost nothing, and in the empty space I make, I have adjusted to a life without a mom and dad. I never had any anyway. My books raised me right and my mirror was the truth. My distorted beliefs, which kept me in dark caves, were put back on the potter's wheel and spun into tall, solid cones that tower into lighted skies. I have lived a lot of life. I know what it feels like to nestle a gun into my father's temple. I know what it feels like to think I'm going to die at the hands of another. I know what it feels like to be cut, caged, or taken and I know what it feels like to escape. I know what it feels like to be trapped in the person they made you into and to break free to be the person you truly are.

And I have come back to God. The essence of God is everywhere. I know it when a ladybug lands on my wrist. Feel it in the teary intense gaze of an old man's adoring eyes. Know it when the sky is set ablaze by fiery colors when it seems as if I, in this harried world, am the only one truly watching.

In my mind's eye, I stand at ocean's edge, arms outstretched and lifted to receive all of the truth, beauty, and love that life can give me. I have finally found my pure white peace.

MY BROTHER AND I CRUISE ALONG the wide open highway, eighty miles an hour on a seamless glide in his cherry red Mustang convertible. The radio coaxes me back into the spacious Midwest and we sing along, my brother and I, to Eddie Vedder growling out "Jeremy." Danny grips the ball shifter; he punches the gas and roars down the highway, just like my father did when he ran. I lean back into my black leather bucket seat, turn my head out the window, and a thick tear squeezes out of one eye and plops down my face. Two of the toughest kids in Ohio, tearing along an empty highway, singing lyrics of a lost childhood out their bitter throats without smile or irony.

I HAVE COME BACK to prosecute my mother, to tell her secrets, to rip from her a veil burnt, sewn, crusted onto her skin. I don't know what shape the process will take, but I have got to stop my mother. Stop her from taking each new girl she lures into her life under a false pretense, an altered last name, a soft initial touch, and lacing her tightly into the appendage she will carry with her from doctor to doctor, like a worn, favored teddy bear or satin-edged security blanket. I have pushed the last bubble of my guilt from out behind the wrinkle of wallpaper. I owe her nothing. I will find the records that showed her Ohio foster care license was revoked; I will find the caseworker that jerked the kids away that day; I will make them run a tracer on my mother's Social Security number. I will save that eleven-year-old girl, that next-generation replica of me. And I will do it all through the back door. Because my mother is not done yet; she never will be.

I pick up the phone and call Children's Services.

ACKNOWLEDGMENTS

My deepest thanks go to Katherine Boyle—agent, friend, confidante—who tirelessly donned a miner's cap and cheerleading pom-poms to guide me through every dark turn along the way. With emotion, I thank Ben, who believed in me, and the authors who raised me with their titles: *I Had It All the Time; Weight Loss for the Mind; The Four Agreements.*

ABOUT THE AUTHOR

Julie Gregory grew up in southern Ohio. She is now an expert writer and spokesperson on Munchausen by proxy and an advocate in MBP cases. A graduate student in psychiatry at Sheffield University, England, she currently lives in the United States. Visit her website at: www.juliegregory.com

———

If you need help or suspect abuse, call Childline on 0800 1111 or the NSPCC Child Protection Helpline on 0808 800 5000 any time of the day or night. Calls are free and anonymous.